Trans Men in Malaysia

Gendering Asian Society, Politics and Development

Gendering Asian Society, Politics and Development is a transdisciplinary book series that offers a distinctive space for monographs and anthologies that explore the multifaceted ways that gender shapes the landscapes of societies, politics, and development in Asia. It lays bare the visible and invisible work of gender and highlights the profound influences of gendering as a critical device and as a hermeneutic in organizing and making sense of contemporary Asia. In examining Asia through a gendered lens, it unsettles the Euro-centric production of gender related knowledges and theories. Our series welcomes a wide variety of perspectives, time frames, geographical outlooks, and methodological approaches.

Series Editor
Dr Xiaodong Lin, University of Warwick
Dr Kailing Xie, University of Birmingham

Editorial Board
Oleg Benesch, University of York
Juanita Elias, University of Warwick
Minwoo Jung, Loyola University, Chicago
Seagh Kehoe, University of Westminster
Sunyhe Kim, Ewha Womans University
Elisabeth Lund Engebretsen, University of Stavanger
Swati Parashar, University of Gothenburg
Shanthi Thambiah, University of Malaysia

Trans Men in Malaysia

Decision-Making, Masculinity, and Manhood

Vizla Kumaresan

Amsterdam University Press

Cover illustration: Erin Malikhain, @alterinate

Cover design: Coördesign, Leiden
Lay-out: Crius Group, Hulshout

ISBN	978 90 4856 259 6
e-ISBN	978 90 4856 260 2 (pdf)
e-ISBN	978 90 4857 276 2 (accessible ePub)
DOI	10.5117/9789048562596
NUR	695

© V. Kumaresan / Amsterdam University Press B.V., Amsterdam 2025

All rights reserved. Without limiting the rights under copyright reserved above, no part of this book may be reproduced, stored in or introduced into a retrieval system, or transmitted, in any form or by any means (electronic, mechanical, photocopying, recording or otherwise) without the written permission of both the copyright owner and the author of the book.

No part of this book may be used or reproduced in any manner for the purpose of training artificial intelligence technologies or systems.

Table of Contents

1.	Introduction	7
	Decision-Making	11
	Be/com/ing Male	13
	References	19

Part 1 You're Not a Boy

2.	Growing Up "Female"	25
	Girls Are Not Boys!	31
	I Am Different?	36
	References	44
3.	Experiencing Femininity	47
	Learning to Be Female	48
	The Force of Culture and Tradition	53
	The Force of Violence	56
	Experiences of Gender-Based Violence	57
	Reminders of the Status of Female	58
	Influences on Decision-Making	62
	References	65

Part 2 I Am a Man, I Guess?

4.	Realising Male Identity	71
	Coming Out and Transitioning	72
	Stages and Transitions	76
	Transitioning in Safety	79
	Passing as Men	83
	Learning to Be Men	86
	References	91
5.	Experiencing Masculinity	95
	Experiencing Relationships with Men	96
	Sex and Masculinity	99
	Feelings and Masculinity	101

Women's Reactions to Trans Men's Masculinity	103
Experiencing Relationships with Women	104
Gender Gatekeeping and Masculinity	108
Gender (In)Equality and Masculinity	109
References	113

Part 3   I Know I Am a Man

6.	Challenging Masculinity	117
	Experiencing Male Privilege	118
	Male Privilege and the Pedestal Effect	120
	Male Privilege and Women	121
	Male Privilege and Men	123
	Challenging Hegemonic Masculinity	126
	Race and the Construction of Gender Relations in Malaysia	128
	Race and the Hegemony of Masculinity in Malaysia	132
	References	138
7.	Rejecting Masculinity?	143
	Embracing the Feminine	144
	Embracing Emotionality	146
	Embracing Femininity, Challenging Masculinity	148
	Embracing Femininity, Experiencing Agency	151
	Imagining a New Manhood	152
	Challenging Stereotypes	157
	Imagining New Ways of Being Men	159
	References	161
8.	Conclusion	163
	References	167
Appendix		169
	Analysing Interviews	169
	Developing Chapter Outlines	169
Index		171

1. Introduction

Abstract: Trans men in Malaysia are an understudied population with a dearth in examination of the construction of their masculine identities. This chapter builds the case for examining masculinities from the lived realities of trans men to draw attention to the specifics of gender relations in conservative and religious Malaysia. In enquiring the psychology of trans men's decision-making, this study asks from where trans men learn about being men, the factors that affect aspects of masculinity they will adopt, the roles played by various institutions in the process of trans men's construction of their masculine identities, and the cognitive factors that go into the decision-making processes in becoming men.

Keywords: trans men, Malaysia, decision-making, masculinities

Much has changed since the publication of Teh Yik Koon's 1998 seminal study on trans women in Malaysia. First, the term "transgender" (including trans women/men) has replaced the use of "transsexual." Teh's work also widely uses the term "cross-dresser" to describe a transgender person, as she does with the term "male transsexual" to refer to trans women. In her study, she suggests that the term transsexual was developed in the West and has come to be accepted and used by Malaysian medical professionals and academics, as many of them were educated in the West. Teh's (1998) study assumes that all transgender people aspire to undergo "sex reassignment surgery," which is now referred to as gender affirmation surgery,[1] thus reifying the use of the term "transsexual" and positioning the identity as a medicalised one. Since that study's publication, the Yogyakarta Principles[2] were drafted in

---

[1]   The term is used to recognise that surgery is not essential to identify as transgender, and that surgeries may be a choice for those who want to alter their body to affirm their gender identity and/or expression.

[2]   The Yogyakarta Principles address a broad range of international human rights standards and their application to SOGIE issues. On 10 November 2017, a panel of experts published additional principles, the Yogyakarta Principles plus 10, expanding on the original document reflecting

---

Kumaresan, Vizla. *Trans Men in Malaysia: Decision-Making, Masculinity and Manhood.* Amsterdam: Amsterdam University Press, 2025.
DOI: 10.5117/9789048562596_CH01

2006 following concerns from human rights experts responding to well-documented patterns of abuse related to sexual orientation and gender identity and expression (SOGIE). The Yogyakarta Principles situate SOGIE as a human rights issue, thus affirming as universal the terms used to describe sexualities and identities. What has not changed since Teh's study more than two decades ago are the issues faced by transgender people in Malaysia.

As of the end of the third quarter of 2023, Malaysia has a population of 33.5 million people (Department of Statistics Malaysia, accessed on 2 January 2024). Malaysia disaggregates population data by race, with 70.1% of the population self-identifying as Bumiputera,[3] 22.6% as Chinese, 6.6% as Indian, and 0.7% identifying as Other (Department of Statistics Malaysia, accessed on 2 January 2024).[4] Statistics on gender are disaggregated by biological sex, whereby the state[5] only recognises male and female as assigned at birth. The data on the primary identity category of Malaysians are race and sex. To date, there is a paucity of national data on transgender people, thus making them invisible. Teh's later study on *mak nyah*s (Teh, 2002)[6] cites data from the Malaysian NGO PT Foundation,[7] working on the issue of HIV/AIDS, that estimate 10,000 trans women in Malaysia. This number is disaggregated by race, whereby 70% are Malay and the rest are Chinese (27.5%), Indians (7.8%), and other minority ethnic groups (14%).

In Malaysia, as identities—including gender expression—closely intersect with race (Wong, 2012), specific terms are assigned to transgender people based on their racial identities. For example, *pengkid* was commonly understood as a term for a masculine-looking Malay-Muslim lesbian (Wong, 2012). Race is also an important identity as the legal tenets outlined in Islam become applicable to Malay-Muslim transgender people. A dual

---

developments in international human rights law and practice since the 2006 principles. The new document also contains 111 "additional state obligations," related to areas such as torture, asylum, privacy, health, and the protection of human rights defenders. The full text of the Yogyakarta Principles and the Yogyakarta Principles plus 10 are available at www.yogyakartaprinciples.org.

3   A term used to describe Malaysians of Malay origin, as well as the Indigenous peoples of Peninsular and East Malaysia.

4   "Others" is a ubiquitous category meant to encompass racial categories of people not identifying as Bumiputera, Chinese, or Indian. This could include people who identify as Sri Lankan Tamil (Ceylonese), Punjabi, or mixed parentage.

5   Throughout this book the use of the term "state" pertains to the governing body of Malaysia, comprising the executive, legislative, and judiciary elements of government.

6   Teh explains that in Malaysia, "transsexuals" generally refers to "male transsexuals," i.e. trans women, referred to as *mak nyah*, and acknowledges that there are "male transsexuals," i.e. trans men, referred to as *pak nyah* that constitute a smaller number of transgender people.

7   PT Foundation was previously known as Pink Triangle.

legal system exists in Malaysia, where Muslims are subject to civil laws (administered at the federal level) and Shariah laws (administered at the state level). The Shariah laws differ across the 13 states in Malaysia. The Human Rights Watch (HRW), in its 2014 study on the state of transgender people in Malaysia, argues that Malaysia is one of the few countries in the world that explicitly criminalises transgender people.

In their report on the state of transgender people in Malaysia, HRW reports that trans women have been historically accepted in Malaysian society. However, this changed with rising Islamisation beginning in the 1980s (Human Rights Watch, 2014). Gender-affirming surgeries were performed by a team of surgeons at the University of Malaya hospital between 1980 and 1982 before a fatwa[8] banning such procedures was issued by the National Fatwa Council. Although a fatwa is not legally binding, the hospital shut down its services in 1983. The HRW report outlines the state's views on trans women, which condones conversion therapy and practices. Advocates for trans women saw them forming a strategic alliance with the federal welfare department, who would provide funds to trans women wanting to start their own small businesses. Yet, the welfare department regarded trans women as a social problem requiring rehabilitation to identify as men as per their sex category.

Julian Lee (2011) explains that the Muslim authorities' focus on policing gender identity and sexual behaviour was an outcome of large social transformations in Malay society since Malaysia's independence in 1957. The changing nature of work and social distribution of wealth saw many people from villages moving into cities to find work in factories. The factories preferred employing young, unmarried women in their late teens or early twenties. Women leaving their homes to live in dormitories or in shared housing in the city no longer lived within the confines of a traditional patriarchal family arrangement. This was also cemented by their earning an income, thus challenging the breadwinning role of their fathers and brothers. Women being far away from kin meant that traditional ways of living that placed the family in a position of control over women's sexuality were usurped. The women were being portrayed in the media as becoming Westernised, having rejected traditional Malay gender traits like shyness and timidity, and as sexually promiscuous. Control over women, therefore, had to be imposed through law. The Islamic Shariah laws were thus seen as important to regulate sexuality when families could not.

---

8   A fatwa is a non-legal binding opinion provided by a qualified scholar of Islamic law in response to a question.

The late 1990s saw LGBT communities come front and centre as the political affairs of the then-ruling party, United Malays National Organisation (UMNO),[9] played out nationally. Following the arrest of then Deputy Prime Minister Anwar Ibrahim under charges of sodomy, a vigilante group called The People's Voluntary Anti-Homosexual Movement (Pasrah) was formed to protect Malaysia from "the disgusting practice of homosexuality" (Human Rights Watch, 2014, p.12). The violence was documented by HRW and by a Malaysian NGO called Justice for Sisters (JFS), and little to no action was taken against perpetrators. Nationally, there was also a clamping down on discourse on sexuality rights. Malaysia can be repressive against non-cis and heteronormative gender identities as well as non-heterosexual sexual practices that occur outside of marriage. This prejudice has become integrated into administrative and legal structures. As with the findings from HRW's study on the state of trans women in Malaysia, Lee (2011) argues that the slide to intolerance has occurred in the context of widespread social and legal Islamisation, which reflects rising conservative Islamic perspectives on gender and sexuality.

In this context of transgender reality in Malaysia, the questions this study[10] seeks to understand concern the experiences of trans men[11] pertaining to their relationship with men and masculinity. There was a dearth of research on trans men in Malaysia when I began working on this study in 2018. Since then, publications on trans men in Malaysia, notably from Sharon Bong (2020a, 2020b) and Joseph Goh (2019, 2020), examine intersections of processes of becoming trans men with religious and national identities. Trans men in Malaysia are aware that there is an inordinate focus on trans women in the literature on transgender people. Some are relieved for the silence surrounding their identities, which allows them to be "stealth,"[12] thus lending them a sense of safety. Others, however, experience this invisibility as marginalisation and oppression due to the silence around the narratives of their lives and the meanings they give to becoming and being men in Malaysia.

This book aims to discover the decision-making processes trans men in Malaysia utilise when constructing their masculine identities. In addressing

---

9   UMNO is a key party in the former ruling coalition, Barisan Nasional, that was in power since Malaysia's independence from 1957 to 2018.

10   This study was completed as a requirement for completion of a PhD programme at Monash University, Malaysia.

11   People assigned female at birth who identify as men.

12   A slang word amongst transgender people to indicate that they are not out as transgender and are perceived as cisgender.

the central question in the book, the study also aims to discover from whom trans men learn about being men, and the role played by various institutions in the process of trans men's construction of their masculine identities. Finally, it aims to explore the factors that influence the aspects of masculinity that trans men adopt. The following two sections will discuss the areas of decision-making and masculine identity and how they relate to each other in this study.

Decision-Making

Decision-making is understood based on the premise of the problem-solving process whereby a person is motivated to avoid psychological distress arising from inconsistencies in the information available to them. Decisions are thus made with the aim of aligning information about a situation or environment. Leon Festinger's (1957) theory of cognitive dissonance proposes that a negative drive state is achieved when a person holds opposing or inconsistent thoughts. Decision-making then seeks to reduce the inconsistencies between incompatible thoughts. Dissonance can occur either at the pre-decision or post-decision stage. Pre-decisional dissonance affects the decisions people will make, while post-decisional dissonance follows a choice that has already been made, and the avoidance or reduction of this dissonance influences later behaviour.

The problem-solving perspective to decision-making is also demonstrated with heuristics, which represent an approach not designed to be perfect but sufficient to reach an immediate goal. Heuristics are mental shortcuts serving to reduce cognitive load while increasing decision-making speed. Representativeness heuristics involve judgements based not on a critical examination of available information but on how similar prospects are to the prototypes a person holds in their mind. Availability heuristics occur when people make judgements about the probability of events by the ease with which examples come to mind. Based on this theory of heuristics, it has been suggested that masculinity is a heuristic (O'Neil et al., 2017) and the reliance on gender roles serves as a convenient form of problem-solving.

Heuristics are not based on available information but on what a person knows or assumes to know, thus giving rise to errors in cognitive processing. One result of such errors is gender role conflict (GRC), which is a psychological state in which socialised gender roles have negative consequences for individuals at four overlapping and complex levels (cognitive, emotional, behavioural, and unconscious) due to restrictive gender roles learned in sexist and patriarchal societies. A social information processing component is then attached to GRC, giving rise to a computational model that includes six cognitive steps that individuals go through to respond to the demands of any given situation. These steps are encoding of cues, interpretation of cues, clarification of goals, response access or construction, response decision, and behavioural enactment.

The influence of GRC on decision-making has been widely explored.[13] While serving to widen narratives of masculinity beyond ideas of traditional manhood, the GRC model does not challenge patriarchal ideas of male power. One study (Bach, 2017) found that the use of GRC did not challenge fears of male subordination in the construction of the masculine self. The GRC has been criticised for being too simplistic a tool in explaining gender and masculinity (Enns, 2008). An obvious issue around the construction of the GRC model is its limited use with and amongst men. The GRC, it would seem, was not intended for women, as its authors (O'Neil et al., 2017) explain that the model was developed to help answer questions as to why men are more likely to become violent in society and in families. The model, through a positivist approach, reifies stereotypes and cultural perceptions of men and masculinities.

A more gender-neutral theory is evident in Albert Bandura's (1986) social cognitive theory, which incorporates human agency in human development, adaptation, and change. It makes the argument that cognitive processes do not function independently from interpersonal factors or self-reflectiveness. People exercise their agency and actively construct behaviours through an interplay between cognitive, social, and personal factors. The underpinnings of social cognitive theory laid the groundwork for theories such as identity-based motivation (IBM) (Nurra & Oyserman, 2018). IBM is a social psychological theory of motivation and goal pursuit that builds on social cognition research to explain when and in which situation people's identities motivate them to act toward reaching their goals. It postulates that people make decisions about themselves based on an idea of their perceived future selves. While not specific to gender, unlike the GRC, social cognitive theory and IBM involve active cognitive processes whereby a person must actively engage with information from their environment as well as what they have come to know and perceive in decision-making.

---

13   For details on studies exploring GRC, Rochlen et al. (2008) studied its use amongst stay-at-home fathers. Bach (2017) studied how narratives of fatherhood and gender equality can be incorporated to widen the repertoire of the masculine gender role to reconstruct ideas of compliance and autonomy.

INTRODUCTION

Few models exist to explain trans men's decision-making. One such model is called embodying a male identity (Vegter, 2013), which has five stages: beginnings, identity searching, realising identity, integrating identity, and self-actualisation. The main identity-forming stage (identity searching) sees the trans man first questioning his identity and then changing his behaviours, which include challenging gender norms. According to this model, the start of the realising identity phase sees trans men pursuing physical changes (e.g. hormone therapy), psychological changes (e.g. increased confidence, masculinisation of emotions), and behavioural changes. They may act in more masculine ways and sometimes overcompensate in this. The trans man moves into a state of self-acceptance upon entering the integrating identity phase and achieves identity security and stability in the self-actualisation phase.

Models like the one proposed in embodying a male identity assume that all trans men (or transgender people) will pursue medical changes. The embodying a male identity model also assumes that the process of becoming is linear and chronological, and builds upon itself in a progressive fashion. Referring to this construction of the self within time as chrononormativity[14] and heterotemporality,[15] Rahul Rao (2020, p. 17) argues that this conception does not take into consideration queer realities that require "feeling backward, anti-futurism and critical utopianism." Also, the construction of the self is not independent of historical or state processes; transgender people, as in Malaysia, for example, experience their processes of becoming within the context of colonial and postcolonial systems and structures that govern and determine the realities of everyday life. In exploring Malaysian trans men's process of becoming within the sociopolitical environment of Malaysia, Goh (2020, p. 5) says that for trans men the "processes of self-actualisation and self-determination towards self-affirmed gender identities must not be understood as the solidification of identity, but as an interminable, unruly, oscillating, unpredictable and ambiguous unravelling of meanings."

Be/com/ing Male

Maleness is typically associated with being male and masculine, which is a concept that has notably been difficult to define. Offering the most widely

---

14   Freeman (2010, p. 3) defines "chrononormativity" as the use of time to organise individual human bodies toward maximum productivity.

15   Rao (2020) uses "heterotemporality" to frame postcolonial discussions of queer sexualities in time and space from the perspective of heterosexuality being the norm.

used concepts to understand masculinity, Raewyn Connell (2005) argues that masculinity (as well as femininity) constitutes a collection of practices and relations between genders. It is not something that men only do (or only men do), but it has significance for their emotional and physical well-being; it is an experience. A model defining masculinity must encompass power relations (patriarchy), production relations (divisions of labour), and cathexis (practices that shape and realise desire). These categories of analysis take into consideration the historical and existing relationships between men and women where men have more social, political, and economic power, and that heterosexuality is an expected norm of masculinity. From this basis, Connell establishes the four types of masculinities which are hierarchically situated: hegemonic, complicit, subordinated, and marginalised.

Connell (2005) has argued that hegemonic masculinity is not a fixed character type, but rather the masculinity that occupies the hegemonic position in a given pattern of gender relations, a position that is always contestable. Hegemonic masculinity is understood as the pattern of practices that allow men's domination over women to continue (2005, p. 76). It embodies men's subordination of women in all segments of public and private life, as well as privileging being able-bodied and heterosexual. Hegemonic masculinities can be constructed that do not correspond closely to the lives of any actual men, but are normative and come with the expectation that all men position themselves in relation to it. It is a model that expresses ideals, fantasies, and desires that men are supposed to aspire to. Hegemonic masculinity has no meaning outside its relationship to emphasised femininity (Messerschmidt, 2019) and other forms of masculinity. Crises in masculinity often arise where femininity expands to include that which was previously assumed to be masculine. Proximity to femininity is thus seen as a threat to masculinity, and it is this aspect which situates other men in a hierarchy.

Complicit masculinity pertains to men who do not embody the ideal of hegemonic masculinity and may even be critical of it, but who benefit nonetheless. Trans men are thought to gain from the patriarchal dividend as they are seen as "moving up the gender hierarchy" and have access to "boy's networks" in the workplace and their labour becomes more valued after transitioning than when they were identified as women (Schilt, 2006). Historically, heterosexual men have dominated over gay men. Gay men, hence, have been thought to constitute an oppressed population that has been subordinated. Last in the hierarchy are marginalised masculinities, which refer to those at the intersections of various social and political groups with less power in a given society. They may represent the intersection of masculinity and racial structures in a society.

Masculinity inevitably conjures up notions of power, legitimacy, and privilege; it often symbolically refers to the power of the state and to uneven distributions of wealth (Halberstam, 1998, p. 2). Hence, an understanding of trans men's identity and any process of identity construction cannot ignore questions of power relations, especially since trans men have to reconcile a proximity to femininity. The position of subordination and marginalisation has an impact on the construction of masculinity for trans men, given the kinds of power and authority that cis men feel entitled to in a patriarchal society.

Yet, analyses of power relations have sometimes been lacking in psychological studies of men and masculinities. Psychological studies consider masculinity as a fixed type, matching the idea of what men (and women) are. Following positivist definitions of masculinity, psychology studies the prevalence of pathology amongst men based on the traits associated with masculinity. The positivist approach also considers gender norms as a binary. The study of masculinities has come to be assumed as the study of men (Ford & Lyons, 2011, p. 3). It is assumed that all masculine behaviours are present only in men and feminine behaviours only in women, without consideration for female masculinity. As the fields of psychology and psychiatry have, until recently, treated transgender identities as pathological, trans men pose challenges to this positivist perspective on gender and identity. Halberstam (2008, p. 15) argues that people assigned as female at birth have been making convincing and powerful assaults on the coherence of male masculinity for well over a hundred years. Yet, difficulties persist in disengaging men from masculinity, leading to suggestions that this is due to conservative and protectionist attitudes by men toward masculinity.

Another criticism levelled at studies of masculinities is that they have come to be focused on the West. Critics (Ford & Lyons, 2012) argue that any discussion of masculinities, especially hegemonic masculinity, in Asia and Southeast Asia must consider the ways in which masculinities are shaped by multiple engagements with imperialism, colonialism, nation-building, and economic development programmes. Calls (Wieringa et al., 2007, p. 4) to go beyond the local/global dichotomy seek to include the transnational to consider ways the local and the global infiltrate each other in constructing gender and its relations. Discourse on masculinities in Southeast Asia must also consider the influence of religious fundamentalism, which is linked to the building of nationalist subjectivities based on the valorisation of patriarchal and heterosexist family values (Wieringa et al., 2007, p. 10). Racial hierarchies (Goh, 2012) and political struggles that have resulted in an exalted Malay-Muslim masculinity (Mohamad, 2010) act to order not only masculinities in Malaysia, but also femininities and other genders.

It is in this context that trans men in Malaysia will be positioned in the analysis to follow in this book. Globally, it is acknowledged that trans men studies have been paid little attention (Hansbury, 2005). There has been a longer acknowledgement of trans women than trans men due to a combination of the politics that prioritised nationalistic ideas of what a man is, and the difficulties in isolation of testosterone in the early days of the field of endocrinology. In Malaysia, also, there is an inordinate focus on trans women with regards to academic and medical research as well as social attention and policy. The field of trans men studies is an emerging one, with a spate of publications since 2020. The current project contributes to this growing field of inquiry by examining the decision-making processes trans men utilise, and evaluating the roles played by race, religion, and nation-making politics in the construction of trans men's identities.

As I sought to examine the decision-making processes trans men in Malaysia utilise in their process of becoming men, I recognised that one limitation was that I could not expect interviewees to name these processes. Nor could I expect them to identify and lay these processes out coherently or cohesively. I needed to make inductions from their narratives about and around the processes. They needed to speak of their selves and reflect on their thoughts. I would then have to analyse the data obtained from participants to examine specific patterns in lived experiences, thoughts, and decision-making, and to identify specific decision-making processes. As such, I decided to approach the research question using a qualitative research methodology.

The induction process I utilised requires researchers to refer to a series of empirical cases to identify a pattern from which to make a general statement. Induction requires creating categories and making conclusions based on data. I conducted face-to-face semi-structured interviews to collect data for this study and then utilised a process of induction from their narratives of self and memories of thoughts. This method is necessary, as argued by Susan Stryker (2019), because it creates intersectional perspectives required to build a transfeminist approach. This approach requires the acknowledgement that each person experiences and understands their gendered sense of self differently. Their sense of being a man or woman or something outside of these identities is an idiosyncratic personal matter related to other attributes of life. As this inquiry seeks to examine trans men's histories in the light of living in Malaysia, their memories will, as Rao (2020) argues, come to reflect or be in contention with national history.

The inductive process I utilised for this inquiry required using a series of empirical cases to identify a pattern from which to make a general statement.

INTRODUCTION

Induction also requires creating categories and making conclusions based on data, thus calling for the use of grounded theory methodology (GTM), which, according to Kathy Charmaz (2008), encourages researchers to remain close to their studied worlds and to develop an integrated set of theoretical concepts from their empirical materials that not only synthesise and interpret them but also show processual relationships. A constructivist GTM approach allows researchers to get as close as they can to the inside of participants' experiences but recognises that they cannot replicate participants' experiences. It theorises the interpretive work that research participants do and acknowledges that the resulting theory is an interpretation (Charmaz, 2008). The theory is dependent on the researcher's view—what is seen and not seen—and on the values that the researcher brings with her.

I used this method to draw from 23 Malaysian trans men's narratives, inviting them to give meaning to their own experiences while allowing me to interpret these using theory.[16] This method was chosen in consideration of the silence around trans men's lived realities, to privilege trans men's voices, and to draw out the nuances of their managing the assumed privileges of identifying as men while being racialised and occupying the precarious position of being transgender in Malaysia. This was done with the ethical consideration of providing visibility while protecting the identities of the trans men informants. They decided for themselves the names[17] by which they would be identified in this study and the amount of identifying information appearing in the completed work. This method was also used to move away from the dominance of medicalising and pathologising discourse on transgender identity (Hines & Sanger, 2010).

I gave much consideration to how my positionality—a cisgender and heterosexual woman, an Indian Malaysian feminist, and an LGBTQ-affirming clinical psychologist—affected the information that the informants provided and how I interpreted it. The data in this study differ from Goh's in terms of how the informants spoke to me. Goh's findings are punctuated with expressions of anger and aggression from his respondents. The informants from this study, in contrast, spoke with a very different tone. I cannot help but wonder if my being a woman and a mental health professional impacted how they spoke to me.

This study also sits within the growing work on trans men in Malaysia that have expanded since the publication of Bong and Goh's research on

---

16   A detailed description of the process is provided in appendix 1.
17   Three respondents, Dorian, Mitch, and Shane, wanted to be referred to by their own names. The others chose their own pseudonyms.

the topic. It highlights the growing space for queer theorising in Southeast Asia, which brings attention to the impact of colonial legacies and postcolonial nation-building on gender and sexuality. Lee (2011) has highlighted the exalted positions inhabited by queer people in pre-colonial Malaya. Since then, Malaya has undergone political transformations to become the postcolonial nation-state of Malaysia today, where queer people exist in precarious states of (in)visibility. Working through the decision-making that trans men make in becoming men in Malaysia highlights how factors such as race and the gender-strict socio-legal systems affect gender, sexuality, and manhood. This allows insights into the psychology of identity development and varying perspectives on trans sexuality and identity from the dominant Western discourse.

With this, the data presented in the preceding chapters are grouped into three sections: part 1 explores trans men's narratives of their lives before transitioning (chapters 2 and 3), part 2 examines their narratives of transitioning (chapters 4 and 5), and part 3 examines trans men reconciling their manhood in Malaysia (chapters 6 and 7). In part 1, first, chapter 2 explores participants' negotiations of identifying as male while being perceived as female. Their expressions of masculinity as children are juxtaposed with their realities of being assigned female at birth and the discipline they experienced in being socialised as female. Then, chapter 3 explores their experiences of gender-based violence and the impact this has on their decision-making about masculinity.

Part 2 starts, in chapter 4, with the exploration of participants' coming out process and weighing it against other models of coming out proposed to explain transgender persons' resolution of their identities. Then, I explore how participants experience being socialised into masculinity and the decision-making processes they utilise at this point in their transitions. Chapter 5 delves into trans men's experiences living as men by examining their relationships with other men and women. This chapter first examines the role played by gender stereotypes in homosocial and heterosocial relationships. Then, the chapter examines trans men's relationships with their female histories in relation to their decision-making about masculinity.

Part 3 explores trans men's experiences as they grow in confidence in their identities as men. Chapter 6, first, explores how they come to recognise, and then reconcile, the male privilege that they now experience because they are men. Living as men also brings them to challenge the idea of what being a man is as they contend that they may never be regarded as "real men" due to their biology. This brings them to question hegemonic masculinity, thus posing a challenge to it being a supposed ideal for men. Then, I interrogate in chapter 7 the decision-making that interviewees embark on upon reconciling their female histories. This allows the trans men to challenge prevalent ideas of masculinity and explore new ways of embodying manhood and masculinities that are reflective of their own values and beliefs instead of societal expectations.

References

Bach, A. S. (2017). The ambiguous construction of nondominant masculinity: Configuring the "new" man through narratives of choice, involved fatherhood and gender equality. *Men and Masculinities, 22*(2), 338–359. https://doi.org/10.1177/1097184X17715494

Bandura, A. (1986). *Social foundations of thought and action: A social cognitive theory.* Prentice-Hall, Inc.

Bong, S. A. (2020a). *Becoming queer and religious in Malaysia and Singapore.* Bloomsbury.

Bong, S. A. (2020b). The power of transformation and transforming power: A Malaysian female-to-male transgender person's narrative. In J. N. Goh, S. A. Bong, & T. Kanantu (Eds.), *Gender and sexuality justice in Asia: Finding resolutions through conflicts* (pp. 139–153). Springer.

Charmaz, K. (2008). *Constructing grounded theory: A practical guide through qualitative analysis.* Sage Publications.

Connell, R. (2005). *Masculinities* (2nd edition). Polity Press.

Department of Statistics Malaysia. (2024, January 2). OpenDOSM. https://open.dosm.gov.my/

Enns, C. Z. (2008). Toward a complexity paradigm for understanding gender role conflict. *The Counseling Psychologist, 36*(3), 446–454. https://doi.org/10.1177/0011000007310974

Festinger, L. (1957). *A theory of cognitive dissonance.* Stanford University Press.

Ford, M., & Lyons, L. (2011). Introduction. In M. Ford & L. Lyons (Eds.), *Men and Masculinities in Southeast Asia* (pp. 1–19). Routledge.

Freeman, E. (2010). *Time Binds: Queer temporalities, queer histories.* Duke University Press. https://doi.org/10.1215/9780822393184

Goh, J. N. (2012). The homosexual threat: Appraising masculinities and men's sexualities in Malaysia. In J. Hopkins & J. C. H. Lee (Eds.), *Thinking through Malaysia: Culture and identity in the 21st Century* (pp. 167–186). SIRD.

Goh, J. N. (2019). Untying tongues: Negotiations and innovations of faith and gender among Malaysian Christian trans men. *Culture and Religion, 20*(1), 1–20.

Goh, J. N. (2020). *Becoming a Malaysian trans man: Gender, society, body and faith.* Palgrave Macmillan.

Halberstam, J. (1998). *Female masculinity*. Duke University Press.

Hansbury, G. (2005). The middle men: An introduction to the transmasculine identities. *Studies in Gender and Sexuality, 6*(3), 241–264. https://doi.org/10.1080/15240650609349276

Hines, S., & Sanger, T. (2010). *Transgender identities: Towards a social analysis of gender diversity*. Routledge.

Human Rights Watch (2014). *"I'm scared to be a woman": Human rights abuses against transgender people in Malaysia*. Human Rights Watch.

Lee, J. C. H. (2011). *Policing sexuality: Sex, society and the state*. Zed Books.

Messerschmidt, J. W. (2019). The Salience of "Hegemonic Masculinity". *Men and Masculinities, 22*(1), 85 – 91. 10.1177/1097184X18805555

Mohamad, M. (2010). Making majority, undoing family: Law, religion and the Islamisation of the state in Malaysia. *Economy & Society, 39*(3), 360–384. https://doi.org/10.1080/03085147.2010.486218

Nurra, C., & Oyserman, D. (2018). From future self to current action: An identity-based motivation perspective. *Self and Identity, 17*(3), 343–364. https://doi.org/10.1080/15298868.2017.1375003

O'Neil, J., Wester, S. R., Heesacker, M., & Snowden, S. J. (2017). Masculinity as a heuristic: Gender role conflict theory, superorganisms, and system-level thinking. In R. F. Levant & Y. J. Wong (Eds.), *The psychology of men and masculinities* (pp. 75–103). American Psychological Association. https://doi.org/10.1037/0000023-004

Rao, R. (2020). *Out of time: The queer politics of postcoloniality*. Oxford University Press.

Rochlen, A.B., Suizzo, M., McKelley, R.A., and Scaringi, V. (2008). "I'm Just Providing for My Family": A qualitative study of stay-at-home fathers. *Psychology of Men and Masculinity, 9*(4), 193 – 206. doi: 10.1037/a0012510

Schilt, K. (2006). Just one of the guys?: How transmen make gender visible at work. *Gender & Society, 20*(4), 465–490. https://doi.org/10.1177/0891243206288077

Stryker, S. (2019). *Transgender history: The roots of today's revolution*. Hachette Book Group.

Teh, Y. K. (1998). Understanding the problem of *mak nyahs* (male transsexuals) in Malaysia. *South East Asia Research, 6*(2), 165–180.

Teh, Y. K. (2002). *The Mak Nyahs: Malaysian male to female transsexuals*. Eastern Universities Press.

Vegter, V. (2013). Conceptualising masculinity in female-to-male trans-identified individuals: A qualitative inquiry. *Canadian Journal of Counselling and Psychotherapy, 47*(1), 88–108.

Wieringa, S. E., Blackwood, E., & Bhaiya, A. (2007). Introduction. In S. E. Wieringa, E. Blackwood, & A. Bhaiya (Eds.), *Women's sexualities and masculinities in a globalising Asia* (p. 4). Palgrave Macmillan.

Wong, Y. (2012). Islam, sexuality and the marginal positioning of *pengkids* and their girlfriends in Malaysia. *Journal of Lesbian Studies, 16*(4), 435–448. https://doi.org/10.1080/10894160.2012.681267

Yogyakarta Principles. (2006). *The Yogyakarta Principles: Principles on the application of international human rights law to sexual orientation and gender identity.* Geneva: United Nations. https://yogyakartaprinciples.org/

Yogyakarta Principles. (2017). *The Yogyakarta Principles plus 10: Additional principles and state obligations on the application of international human rights law in relation to sexual orientation, gender identity, gender expression and sex characteristics to complement the Yogyakarta Principles.* Geneva: United Nations. https://yogyakartaprinciples.org/

Part 1

You're Not a Boy

2. Growing Up "Female"

Abstract: In enquiring how trans men make decisions about the kind(s) of masculinity they want to express, 23 in-depth semi-structured interviews were examined. Centring the experiences of trans men and the meanings they give to masculinity and masculine identities reveals three distinct stages of decision-making. This chapter deals with the first aspect whereby trans men deal with cognitive dissonance arising from conflict between what they describe as their true selves and having been assigned female at birth. Here they indicate that they were not socialised as boys, yet expressed masculine behaviours. The chapter then explores how they come to fully experience the discrepancy between their assigned sex and their gender identity upon realising that their bodies are that of females, when they are told by others that they are female, and when they experience puberty.

Keywords: trans men, Malaysia, decision-making, cognitive dissonance, gender expression

Upon birth, Malaysian citizens are granted a certificate that contains the child's name, the name of their parents, religious identity, race, and sex.[1] The child's religious identity and race are usually based on the fathers' unless they are Muslim, where there is no choice. The child's sex is determined by its external genitalia and is assigned either male or female. The trans men interviewed for this study describe their experiences of identifying as male while being assigned female at birth in the Malaysian registration system, which challenges their narratives of a natural[2] identity. The narrative of

---

1   The newborn's birth certificate can only be issued if the parents can provide a marriage certificate.

2   This finding is in contrast with Green's (2005), whose study shows that trans men only knew they were masculine when they were told so by others. In Green's (2005) study, "non-trans men" report that an internal understanding is their primary source of information that they are men. Five out of the nine trans men in Green's (2005) study reported that they felt different from girls or women. In my study, all the trans men reported feeling different from girls or women.

Kumaresan, Vizla. *Trans Men in Malaysia: Decision-Making, Masculinity and Manhood.* Amsterdam: Amsterdam University Press, 2025.
DOI: 10.5117/9789048562596_CH02

naturalness comes from expressing only masculine traits as children and ascribing the expression to something they could feel but not name. As explained by the Yogyakarta Principles from 2006, gender identity[3] is separate from gender expression.[4] Separating these concepts reveals the different facets each brings to ideas of oneself and the decisions that one makes regarding living and portraying that identity. The separation of the two concepts also means that gender identity and gender expression are independent of each other, yet it is assumed that they are interdependent, i.e. a person assigned male at birth will see themselves as a boy/man and be masculine. Hence, one can express masculine or feminine traits without identifying as either male or female.

Gender identity is felt intrinsically while gender expression is acted out or performed. This is evident in the way trans men speak about their expressions of masculinity as children. Jameel, a 35-year-old[5] Malay trans man who identified as an ex-Muslim, spoke of his childhood as such:

> My brother had a circumcision [ceremony]. I [told] my mom I wanted that. [In] Malay [culture] when a boy [is] a certain age [they] have to go through a circumcision [ceremony]. When I saw my brother laying down and everything, I just asked my mom when [was] my turn.

Identifying as an ex-Muslim, Jameel felt no affinity for his Malay identity. However, he grew up with influences from both, as the identities of Malay and Muslim are inextricably intertwined in Malaysia. Growing up with a brother and a sister, he said he was always closer to his brother and assumed he would also experience the circumcision ceremony that was held for his brother. As a child, he engaged in play such as "climbing trees, dig[ging] up soil and destroying stuff," and playing football, and he preferred boys' clothes that his mother would buy for him. He described being happy at this time as he got "to live who I wanted to be."

---

3   "Gender identity," as defined by the Yogyakarta Principles, refers to each person's deeply felt internal and individual experience of gender, which may or may not correspond with the sex assigned at birth, including the personal sense of the body (which may involve, if freely chosen, modification of bodily appearance of function by medical, surgical, or other means) and other expressions of gender, including dress, speech, and mannerisms.

4   "Gender expression," as defined by the Yogyakarta Principles, refers to each person's presentation of the person's gender through physical appearance—including dress, hairstyles, accessories, and cosmetics—and mannerisms, speech, behavioural patterns, names, and personal references, noting further that gender expression may or may not conform to a person's gender identity.

5   The ages of interviewees are as of the date of interviews, between September and December 2019.

GROWING UP "FEMALE"

Jameel's use of the phrase "live who I wanted to be" reflects the experience of coherence between gender identity, which is felt deeply, and gender expression reflected in mannerisms and behaviour patterns. Like Jameel, many trans men talked about being their "real selves" likened to a need to be authentic[6] to themselves and the world. Being authentic is a process requiring discovering, developing, constructing, and maintaining a core sense of self through a variety of mental and behavioural processes. For trans men like Jameel, their core selves are male, and they organise their thoughts, feelings, and behaviours in accordance with what they perceive as that identity. In concordance with this, Jameel wanted to experience a procedure that would mark his body as male. Male circumcision is a religious rite that Muslim boys undergo. It is a tradition predating Islam and there is an argument that it is not a compulsory ritual (Rizvi et al., 1999, p. 13). There are differing views about male circumcision among the six different schools of law in Islam, and only the Shafi'i school considers it compulsory (*wajib*). As Islamic affairs in Malaysia are based on interpretations from the Shafi'i school (Nornajwa, 2016), the ritual is, therefore, *wajib* for Muslim boys and men. It is not just a religious rite but a symbol of passage into adulthood, and circumcision ceremonies are even conducted publicly in Malaysia. Jameel's wanting the circumcision experience is symbolic of him wanting to be affirmed as a male.

Like Jameel, other trans men described a sense of connection to their gender identities during childhood. This suggests that they express behaviours that are in harmony and aligned with that identity. Blue was 26 years old and identified as Chinese Malaysian. He was employed as an interior designer. Explaining his childhood behaviours, he said:

> There would be people fishing outside the school. They would just [go] there and fish [for] crabs. I [would be] very curious. I [would walk] down to the swamp and try to catch the crabs for them. And then people would say, "this is not a girl thing to do," "this is how a boy will behave." But I [didn't] understand what [that meant]. I would always do things like that.

Blue's childhood memories were of being reprimanded for the type of play that he preferred, which was thought to be masculine. About being told

---

6   Bostan (2016, p. 56) argues that being authentic means "acting accordingly to a harmonious way of life, one in which [there is] comfortable congruency between one's thoughts, feelings, emotions and behaviours." Kernis & Goldman (2006, p. 294) define "authenticity" as "the unobstructed operation of one's true- or core-self in one's daily enterprise."

to behave like a girl, Blue said, "I did not know how to [differentiate] if it's a boy thing, or it's a girl thing. It [was] playful and I [would] go out most of the time, more adventurous and curious, that I would [be active]." His concerns were less about being masculine than about having an affinity for the outdoors. That he was being masculine only became evident to him when others pointed it out. Blue described going on school camping trips and being housed with female students. On one of these trips, a female student's shoe fell down a slope. The girls thought they should call on the male students to get the shoe. Without thinking about it, Blue went down the slope and retrieved it for her. Following this incident, he was told by the female students that he was "manly," and it made him happy, although he did not understand why that act was perceived as unusual.

By ascribing the narrative of "natural" to his behaviours, he is assuming a view that a separation of the sexes—male and female—is natural, and his behaviours stemmed from that naturalness. Feminists (Budgeon, 2003) have challenged the question of what is natural when it comes to sex and gender. Taking for granted the notion of naturalness legitimises a system of structured inequality. Questioning this naturalness leads to a more social constructionist view of gender. However, juxtaposed to this is the question of where a child's notion of play comes from. While feminists have rightly contested this idea of naturalness, child psychologists and scientists have raised questions to suggest otherwise (Kilvington & Wood, 2016, p. 36). Developmental scientists and psychologists have shown that play is an emergent activity that is not learnt. Children do not learn from their elders how to play but develop and construct it by and for themselves. Play itself, it is argued, is not gendered, but children's ideas about gender emerge from their play. By this view, it is not the children's gender identity that determines what or how they play but how they play that influences gender.[7]

The idea of gender emerging from play can also be seen in LaudeB's telling of how he displayed masculine behaviours when he was a child. LaudeB was 34 years old and worked as a shift leader. He is Indian Malaysian and grew up with his sister, his mother, and extended family. He said he

---

7   Studies on play in Malaysia demonstrate that play is highly determined by concerns for children's physical activity instead of social and cognitive development (Ismail et al., 2015), the pedagogical value of play (Abu Bakar et al., 2015), and children's safety (Ilmi et al., 2018), suggesting a degree of adult supervision over children's play. However, Agha et al. (2019) demonstrate that children display agency in accessing play spaces, thus extending and expanding their lived spatial, temporal, social, and imagined geographies.

GROWING UP "FEMALE"

was surrounded by many women while growing up. Speaking about his childhood, he told me:

> So growing up I [was] never girlish. I have always been how boys are seen by society. And I dressed up boyishly. I have always never liked dresses. I tried to burn them from the time I was three years old. I used to stand and pee. I used to play with boys' toys. I used to cut Barbie dolls. I don't know why they'd give me Barbie dolls [I would] cut her hair. Cut her head. Cut the hand. Break the leg. I know [it is] violent but yeah. I guess I was frustrated because I wanted more of the cars [and] guns. I'd be happy if someone bought me a gun. But they were all buying me dolls. So I'd be frustrated. When I was in kindergarten I never mixed with the girls. I always mixed with the boys. It felt right to be with them. Running around and playing *Street Fighter* and all that stuff with them.

In LaudeB's depiction of his behaviours as a child, he understood only that he did not like to play with dolls which were considered girls' toys. The Barbie dolls he played with are also highly feminine dolls, displaying emphatic femininity (Rogers, 1999, p. 14), and have been criticised for setting an extreme and unsustainable standard of femininity. Even when Barbie is supposed to be displaying masculinity, she is feminine (Rogers, 1999, p. 14); whether Barbie is dressed in a police uniform or as a tradesperson, she is unmistakably feminine.[8] LaudeB could not connect or play with Barbie dolls, as playing with them was in opposition to his identity as male. Evidence[9] suggests that boys and girls demonstrate preferences for playmates of the same or other sex depending on their age (Kilvington & Wood, 2016, p. 36). However, if they are particularly interested in play that is typical of their own sex, they would initiate different forms of play depending on how they view male and female and how they fit within these ideas (Kilvington & Wood, 2016, p. 38). Children engage in forms of play which are consistent with their own gender identity, a trend displayed by Blue and LaudeB.

Studies on children and play present evidence that gendered play differences are universal. They assume and reiterate that boys play outdoors

---

8   Rogers (1999, p. 14) notes, "Nothing about her appearance ever looks androgynous or gender neutral."

9   Kilvington & Wood cite evidence from developmental science, neuroscience, and psychology suggesting that, as children, boys and girls choose to play at and with different things and in different ways. At the age of about three or four, they tend to choose more play partners from their own sex than the other. These findings should be taken with caution as most studies on children and play take place in playgrounds which are social spaces that are highly gendered.

and in large groups, while girls play indoors and participate more in talking and discussion. Boys are more physical and engage in rough-and-tumble kinds of play. Girls, on the other hand, engage in dress-up play where they can be glamorous. Trans men repeat these ideas in their telling of their childhood experiences. For example, Jake, a 30-year-old Chinese Malaysian who worked in the logistics industry, described his play preferences as more masculine, although he had opportunities to socialise with girls. Speaking about his childhood play, he said:

> I do sports. I'm a very sporty person. So basically I play rough sports like the guys. It's easier to tell [you] what I didn't do as a female more than what I did as a guy because basically I did nearly everything you can imagine of a guy. Playing [with] Barbie dolls was not something that I did. Gossiping with girls, pillow talk [were] not [things] I would do. I would just fall asleep [at sleepovers]. I would play and of course where else everyone would start talking and I don't know playing [with] dolls and putting [on] makeup, comparing mascara and stuff like that. Things like this I didn't do. Jump into the river [and] catch a fish [I would do] things that you would think of a *kampung*[10] boy doing.

Jake's description of attempting to "do as female" by actively choosing when and when not to participate in activities with female friends, marks these decisions as intentional and effortful. When Jake said it was easier to talk about what he did not do as female rather than what he did as male, he is referring to his doing gender (West & Zimmerman, 1987), specifically how he did not do femininity. Doing gender requires people to convincingly portray masculinity or femininity to be accepted as members of society. Candace West and Don H. Zimmerman (1987) distinguish between sex, sex category, and gender. Sex is social, assigned based on socially accepted norms of biology based on primary and secondary sex characteristics. The category of sex is achieved through applying sex criteria—displays of socially prescribed behaviours and characteristics to proclaim membership in either one of the categories. One's sex category presumes one's sex. Gender refers to the management of conduct in different situations with consideration of normative expectations of sex category. Gender expression is that which bolsters claims to membership in a sex category.

While playing with dolls or make-up are not explicitly feminine behaviours, participating in these activities with his female friends would have

---

10   The Malay word referring to a traditional Malaysian village.

GROWING UP "FEMALE"

indicated that Jake was one of them. West & Zimmerman (1987, p. 126) argue that doing gender, like play, is emergent as an "outcome and a rationale for various social arrangements and as a means of legitimating one of the most fundamental divisions of society." Gender emerges out of social interactions and environments and is perpetuated through daily interactions where people will organise their behaviours to reflect their gender. When Jake said, "It's easier to tell [you] what I didn't do as a female," he was able to recognise certain behaviours as being in the domain of girls/feminine. His resistance to engaging in these activities was resisting being seen as female.

Another example of trans men doing gender can be seen in Dante's description of his experience in school. Dante was 21 years old and described his behaviour as, "I'm the one who's often like acting *lasak*[11] and acting all tough and stuff, protecting all the girls. That's just me I guess." In describing what he thought was his natural tendency to "protect" girls and step in when fights broke out at his primary school,[12] Dante said that the female students expressed their admiration for his boyish behaviour, and boys never bullied him.

Girls Are Not Boys!

Dante was thinking of masculinity in terms of heuristics. Heuristics rely not on critical examinations of available information to form judgements but on how similar prospects are based on ideas that they already have in their minds (O'Neil et al., 2017). Dante already had an idea of masculinity, and his stopping the fight and "protecting all the girls" were consistent with that idea. Dante's description in the quote above is a demonstration of how he, like Jake, was doing gender; he becomes a protective male towards his female classmates. Doing this establishes his gender identity as male and, consequently, establishes a gender binary (Butler, 1999) which posits that there are two sexes resulting in two genders which are the opposite of each other—male/female, protector/ protected—where males protect, and females are protected. Where there are binaries, there also emerges a hierarchy that places higher value on one over the other. Dante believes that he proved himself as strong and superior when he said that the other boys did not dare to bully him.

Dante's reaction to his own behaviour in stopping the fight was one of pride. He saw his behaviour as being consistent with his male identity.

---

11   The Malay word referring to being active or rugged.
12   Primary school is for children ages 7 (standard 1) to 12 (standard 6).

Others' reactions of surprise and awe were unexpected for Dante because, as someone assigned as female, he was expected to behave in ways that affirmed his femininity. Like the other female students, he was expected to be afraid of the situation and wait for someone with more authority, i.e. boys or teachers, to step in for his safety. When others commented on his behaviour, there was already an acknowledgement of the misalignment of his assigned sex and gender expression.

Dante also told me that not all students were receptive to his expressions of masculinity. Some of the female students reprimanded him for behaving like a boy. This was also a common experience amongst the other trans men and this reprimanding disrupted their male self-image, as seen in Dorian's depiction of his childhood. He was a 32-year-old Indian Malaysian. When discussing his childhood, he said:

> Before primary school I was very boyish. I would try and pee like a boy. Standing up and also making it like into an arch when you pee. We didn't have toilet bowls. This was a pre-war house [where there was a squatting toilet]. There was a separate space to bathe and then the toilet. You push things aside and you just do it. My grandmother would see that and [tell me to] pee like a girl.

It was mainly Dorian's grandmother, and not his uncle who lived in the same house, who would chide him to "behave like a girl." Sandra Bartky (1990) describes this kind of policing of females as a form of disciplining that affirms women's lower status in society. Parents, teachers, and members of society take on the role of the disciplinarian in reminding females to behave in ways that do not challenge the gender hierarchy that situates them lower than males. Like the other trans men, Dorian ascribed this masculine behaviour as coming automatically and spontaneously. He told me he had not observed men urinating, was never taught to urinate standing up, and did not recognise that he had to urinate while sitting or squatting because he was assigned female. When his grandmother told him to sit while urinating, Dorian said he "was confused ... uncomfortable." Struggling to explain this, he told me, "I find it hard to explain why I didn't realise it before," referring to his being assigned female at birth because even when he started attending school and had to wear the girls' uniform, use the female toilets, and be grouped with girls for activities, he never doubted his male identity.

While Dorian was reprimanded for expressing masculine behaviour, others experienced different kinds of policing of their behaviours. Dante

GROWING UP "FEMALE"

always had difficulty fitting in with girls. He could tell he was expected to be like them because he recognised that he was wearing the same clothes as them. The hijab[13] that he had to wear became a signifier of and conformity to femininity. The hijab was meant to signal to him that he was assigned female and coercion to wear it was a tool to socialise him into behaving like a girl. Yet, he did not identify as a girl and, at that point, had not quite realised his male identity. Being active and rough (*lasak*) and taking on the role of protecting the girls from other boys' behaviours were ways for him to separate himself from the female identity.

In Malaysia, the hijab plays a prominent role in Muslim women's identity. A study conducted by the Malaysian Muslim-feminist NGO Sisters in Islam (SIS) (Sheriff et al., 2019) showed that 88% of the Muslim women they surveyed believe they have the right to decide if they want to wear the hijab or not. Whilst 62% of the women surveyed said that it is acceptable for Muslim women not to don the hijab, 90% of the respondents believed that women must wear the hijab. These contradictory results show the contested status of the hijab in Malaysia. Muslim women in Malaysia experience social pressure to don the hijab. Malaysian media have reported multiple instances of female Muslim celebrities who face scrutiny on social media, either encouraging them to wear the hijab or criticising them for removing it (Tan, May 8 2019; Looi, 14 January 2020; Tan, 12 June 2020). In April 2019 (Zurairi, 17 April 2019), an event to launch a book on Malaysian Muslim women's experiences of removing their hijab (dehijabbing) was investigated by the Islamic authorities from the state of Selangor after the event garnered negative attention on social media. SIS (2019, p. 35) states that the hijab is tied to pressures women, more than men, are subjected to for the "need to protect an image of the 'proper Muslim woman,' not for self-satisfaction, but to avoid negative perception that others may have." The hijab in Malaysia has significant patriarchal values and meanings attached to it. It is deemed compulsory for women, as women are meant to cover their "intimate parts," i.e. *aurat*.

In contrast, Leila Ahmed's (2017, p. 343) notion of hybrid agencies shows how, for some women, donning the hijab or veil is also "in effect performatively enacting their rejection of both the patriarchal and colonial narratives of the veil." They add on personal and political meanings to the veil although they are fully cognisant of how it has been read not only by men but also by white men (and women). However, where Dante is concerned, the hijab remains an oppressive reminder of his sex assigned at birth, and his resistance to wearing it becomes an act of denying his assigned female identity.

13 Headscarf worn by Muslim women.

Kyle and Hans had experiences similar to Dante's where clothes were tools of signifiers of their identities as females. Kyle was a 30-year-old Chinese Malaysian working in the food industry. While growing up, he did not realise that he was not a boy and could not understand hating dressing in girls' clothes. When he was made to wear a dress, Kyle said: "I cried. I think it was Chinese New Year. I think my mom made me wear a dress and I cried. I didn't want to go out. And then she [conceded and let me] change." Kyle already knew he preferred boys' clothes and did not like wearing any kind of girl's clothes. It was mainly his mother who pushed him towards behaving in more feminine ways, but his father also occasionally stepped in to police his behaviours and dressing. His father called him when he was attending university abroad to reprimand him about shaving his head after he saw a picture of it on Facebook. His father thought that Kyle should have his hair long so that he would "look like a girl." Kyle always managed to find ways to continue expressing his masculinity and, as he grew older, could defend his gender expression despite his parents' resistance.

Hans also talked about dressing in boys' clothes. He was a 29-year-old Malay Malaysian working in the finance industry. His masculine expressions were tolerated by his parents until he reached puberty. He said:

> I think for some time my younger sister kind of thought that I was a brother until she understood the whole thing. My sisters are always in gowns or stuff like that but I would always be in trousers like my brothers. I think my parents didn't really mind how we dressed up. I could just pick whatever I wanted.

Hans's parents allowed him to wear trousers until he reached puberty. His mother then began reprimanding him to be feminine. He explained that "that's when my mom was like you should stop this. You shouldn't be doing this because you're a girl. And she kept on reminding me that."

There is general adult tolerance for the girl child's male expression, also known as tomboyism. Henry Rubin (2003, p. 97) demonstrated that the tomboy identity amongst people assigned female at birth is tolerated with an "implicit normative expectation that the child will grow out of it." It is assumed and accepted that many people whose gender identity is female do express masculine behaviour when they are children and then develop more feminine behaviours as they grow older. Female tomboyism is assumed to be a passing or temporary condition. This is also evident in the experiences of trans men. It was expected that, at some point, Kyle and Hans would

GROWING UP "FEMALE"

grow out of their masculine behaviour expression and start displaying more feminine behaviours like their sisters did.

In an examination of female masculinity, Halberstam (1998, p. 5) explained that tomboyism is a description of "an extended period of childhood female masculinity … for girls and does not generally give rise to parental fears." The "hysterical responses" to feminine expression amongst boys that are not expressed when girls express masculine behaviours exemplify how the latter is tolerated. Tomboyism is associated with a "natural" desire amongst girls for freedoms and mobilities enjoyed by boys. It is meant to signify independence and self-motivation as long as it is associated with a stable identity of being a girl. It is acceptable as the child is at the precipice of experiencing "blossoming womanhood," where tomboyism represents a resistance to adulthood but not femininity, and punished when there is a transgression to signal male identity. Kyle's parents indulged his childhood desire to dress in masculine clothes but chastised him for shaving his head when he was a young adult, which was a signal that Kyle was actively denying his female identity. Tomboyism is also tolerated until puberty, as was Hans's experience, where it is expected that the girl child will accede to performing femininity aligned with her progress to womanhood.

Like Kyle, Damon, a 21-year-old Indian Malaysian university student, experienced pushback from his parents when he wanted to express his masculine identity through dress. Reinforcement that he was not a boy came from his father. He reported that his father would make deals with him to temper his preferred masculine expression. He said:

> There was one year we went to Langkawi.[14] He did not let me pack any boy's clothes. And I was so upset. Because I had to grow my hair out and I had to wear pink the whole time I was there. And pants that had flowers and pink shoes. I was about 8 or 9 years old? I was very much vocal already at that point. I didn't want to wear girls' clothes. I didn't want to touch my sisters' toys. I wanted to have my own toys. I liked to hammer things. I liked tools and guns and swords. And he always had a problem with it. But he's like ok you want to do this. Fine. But you do your part. Every Deepavali[15] you better buy at least five sets [of traditional female attire].

Damon was expected to perform femininity as exemplified by wearing clothing in pink and with flowers. Afraid of his father for the violence he

---

14   An island in the northeast coast of Malaysia which is also a popular tourist destination.
15   The festival of lights celebrated by Hindus.

inflicted on him, his mother, and sisters, Damon felt compelled to listen to his father's demands. Damon's father was exerting control over his gender expression, thus treating him as a docile body, which Michel Foucault (1977, p. 136) explains is one that may be "subjected, used, transformed and improved." Where Foucault's discussion of the docile body (imagined as a man's) is limited to how it is subjected to by the powers of the state, Bartky (1990) explores the impact of patriarchy on bodies that are not biologically male. Bartky (1990, p. 65) argues that there are specific kinds of discipline enacted on female bodies: those that aim to produce a body of a certain size and general configuration, those that bring forth from the body a specific repertoire of gestures, postures, and movements, and those directed toward the display of the body as an ornamented surface. In doing all three of these, Damon's father was exercising disciplinary power to produce in Damon a specific kind of feminine identity and expression, one that he deemed appropriate. This female identity must present with a particular kind of look and conform to her role as inferior to a male authority. Damon's resistance to his father's disciplinary power is because he does not identify as a girl and he refuses to conform to his father's notion of male authority and power. These are aspects that will come to play a significant role in his later decision-making about his own masculinity.

Through separating gender identity and gender expression, I demonstrated in this section how trans men experience a male identity from which they express masculine behaviours. The psychology and development of children's play leads to the idea that gendered behaviours emerge from relational play. In making sense of the gender identities as children, trans men described their engagement in masculine forms of play, standing while urinating, and dressing in boys' clothes were ways that they performed gender as male, and they were reprimanded to behave like girls. Being made to wear girls' clothes, dress in pink, or donning the hijab serves to challenge their male gender identity and expression, resulting in repercussions from their family and social environments that they are not male.

I Am Different?

Trans men's experience of inconsistency between what they know of themselves and how others perceive them results in cognitive dissonance. Festinger (1957) developed the concept to describe psychological arousal caused by inconsistencies between beliefs, behaviours, and external

GROWING UP "FEMALE"   37

information. This state of arousal can be a physical experience whereby the sympathetic nervous system is stimulated, resulting in accelerated heart rate and increased blood pressure, amongst other effects (Robinson & Demaree, 2007). The trans men I spoke to for this study first experienced cognitive dissonance regarding their gender identity when they received information that contradicted their own knowledge of themselves as being male. There are three distinct points at which they experienced this dissonance: (1) when they noticed their genitalia differed from other males, (2) when they were told they were female, and (3) when they experienced puberty.

The trans men first noticed their genitalia when they compared it with that of other children. This happened to Hans, who grew up in a family with two sisters and three brothers. He said:

> I think the first time I realised that I was not a boy was when I was showering with two cousins. I don't remember my age [but it was before I started school]. My *Mak Long*[16] was bathing us. And that's when I noticed that we're different.

This shower incident, for Hans, was an experience of cognitive dissonance as it posed to him an inconsistency between his beliefs, behaviours, and information from his environment. Other times he experienced this inconsistency were when others told him that he was not a boy, or when he was told that he was a girl. This was the case for White Lotus, a 23-year-old Indian Malaysian who identifies as a Catholic Malayalee. He did not identify as male until he was 21 years old. However, when he was younger, he felt uncomfortable at being identified as female. He recounted experiences from his childhood, saying:

> Being called a woman made me feel really out of place because like when people call me a woman I'll be like I should be proud of it. I shouldn't feel like I'm not proud of it. I have female genitalia and I grew up in a family where being a woman is something that you should be proud of. When [someone calls] me a woman I'd just be there sitting and thinking, is that the right pronoun? When someone called me a boy I would immediately feel over the moon. But when my parents [corrected them for calling me a boy] it felt like why [are] you correcting them? Don't correct them because they are right. If they don't know I'm a woman you don't have to correct them.

16   The Malay term for the oldest aunt.

White Lotus's experienced cognitive dissonance because he knew he was not female, but his experience of his body, as he had "female genitalia," was contrary to that knowledge. At that point, he was not yet aware of himself as a trans man, and, therefore, he did not recognise that he was experiencing gender dysphoria (APA, 2014).[17] Gender dysphoria is a reference to the conflict between a person's physical or assigned gender and the gender with which he/she/they identify, and can result from the person being uncomfortable with their body or being uncomfortable with the expected roles of their assigned gender (APA, 2014).

White Lotus's confusion was also caused by the messages he received from his family about womanhood. He was attracted to women but was uncomfortable being called a lesbian: "I did [identify as a woman then]. But calling me lesbian was really out of place [because] every time someone would call me a lesbian I'd immediately take a step back. I'd be like what?" White Lotus attended an all-girl school, where he was socialised as female. At this girls' school, he was trained to be an "empowered woman" capable of standing up for herself without having to be dependent on others, especially men. While he identified as a woman, he had difficulties fitting in with the female students and could not understand why he could not relate to his fellow schoolmates. At first, he identified as "dyke" (masculine-identifying lesbian), but he could not fit in with dyke-identifying females at his school as he was considered too masculine. He also struggled to fit in with other Indian students. He said, "When my friends started realising I was different, I couldn't really get along with everyone." He experienced adolescence as a period of loneliness and estrangement from his peers. He endured a combination of social withdrawal because of depression and social ostracisation that he experienced at school. This experience seems to be consistent with findings (Rubin, 2003) of trans men as unable to fully participate as men in social situations which are gendered.

Others identified White Lotus as lesbian because they perceived him as female, and that was the only way they could make meaning of his sexual attraction. The term also served to mark White Lotus as "different." Assumptions of heterosexuality expect bodies, gender, and desire to be stable, intelligible, and coherent. Thus, a person's sexuality is meant to be directly

---

17   The APA describes gender dysphoria as the psychological distress "when there is a difference between one's experienced or expressed gender." The move from the term gender identity disorder (GID) to gender dysphoria in the *Diagnostic and Statistical Manual of Mental Disorders* (5th edition) (*DSM5*) marks a significant moment in psychiatry and psychology where gender identity itself is no longer pathologised.

GROWING UP "FEMALE" 39

inferred from their sex assigned at birth, as a "stable sex [is] expressed through a stable gender" (Butler, 1999, p. 208). Butler (1999, p. 208) called this the heterosexual matrix, which provides a "grid of cultural intelligibility" that extends to sex/gender/desire where if one is born female, one is expected to be gendered feminine and desire the opposite sex. This is how some bodies "make sense" whilst others do not.

The heterosexual matrix carries with it the heterosexualisation of desire, i.e. the compulsion to desire only the opposite sex. One's sexuality is always assumed to be heterosexual, as it is a compulsory outcome of this configuration. White Lotus's interest in women further challenged the heterosexual matrix because the female students at his school assumed his assigned sex at birth as aligned with his gender expression and sexual attraction. Hence, White Lotus was expected to be sexually attracted to cisgender men (who are also assumed to be heterosexual), but when he displayed an interest in women, his female peers could only make sense of this contravention of the heterosexual matrix by labelling White Lotus lesbian, hence deviant.

The assumed deviance of the label lesbian is also seen in Dines's experience. He was a 32-year-old Indian Malaysian working as a trainer. He said:

> They used to make fun of [my attraction to women]. Oh you like girls you are lesbian you know those type of remarks. At that point of time I didn't know what lesbian meant. Later on I figured [that] lesbian means a female [who] likes another female. When I knew the meaning I got upset [because] I felt like I'm not that.

Dines's parents had never reprimanded him for his expression of masculine behaviour and he was never pushed to be feminine. Being called lesbian at school was his first experience of being socially disciplined for his masculine gender expression. Dines, like White Lotus, challenged the heterosexual matrix when he displayed his attraction towards women, thus becoming the focus of other students' jibes. This kind of social punishment is an example of how trans men are socialised as female and coerced into conforming to the heterosexual matrix. Dines's and White Lotus's attraction to females became a focus of attention from others because they were assigned female at birth and were expected to comply with the expectation that they be attracted to males. Others thus saw it as their duty to correct Dines and White Lotus through punishment in the form of teasing or bullying. The goal of the teasing and bullying was to make Dines and White Lotus comply with the assigned order of being attracted to males as they were read as females, and thus feminine.

The third situation in which trans men realised the discrepancy between their identity and their assigned sex was at the onset of puberty. Dorian explained that he was oblivious to messages that he was assigned female at birth. He talked about his experiences in a co-ed[18] school where he was grouped with female students and briefed on issues such as the appropriate way to dispose of sanitary napkins. Yet, he did not recognise that he was assigned female. Thus, he was shocked when he got his first period:

> I was already starting to develop my chest but I really didn't understand what was happening. By then I already knew about periods and all but it never occurred to me that I would get it too. Sometimes in school someone would have thrown their pad in the toilet and [school authorities] will round us up and be like who threw this? I should have known actually. But when it happened it was a bit of a shock.

Dorian had already known about periods as he was briefed by his grandmother and mother and had attended talks about female reproduction and puberty at school. Although this was a signal that he was assigned female at birth, Dorian explained that he did not understand that it was something that could happen to him. When he saw blood in his underwear, he said, "I asked my mum about it. She was super excited. She was over-excited. She [said] join the club and wow. That made me feel so fucked up. I think I burst into tears. I just felt terrible." Not knowing then that he had a strong internal sense of being a boy, Dorian did not even understand why he felt so bad about the period. His mother's response to knowing that he had gotten his period was one of affirmation as her child had entered womanhood. Though much celebrated, many women experience a sense of ambivalence about their menstruation related to the mixed messages they receive about it. The onset of menstruation marks a girl child's passage into womanhood, which is a milestone of pride, yet she must hide her bleeding from the world (Young, 2005). While she is expected to become proud of her developing body's reproductive and sexual powers, she is also expected to feel disgust and shame over her bodily processes. The experience of puberty is thus already mired in confusion akin to cognitive dissonance. This experience would be heightened for a young trans man experiencing dysphoria regarding his body and identity.

Puberty is an especially significant event for transgender people. It is a physical reminder that their assigned sex is different from how they perceive

18   Common term used in Malaysia to denote mixed-sex schools.

GROWING UP "FEMALE"

themselves. Many trans men report experiencing dysphoria for the first time during puberty as it dawns on them that they are not the boys they thought they were (Rubin, 2003). The ensuing bodily changes following puberty—growing breasts, rounding hips—make it harder for trans men to maintain their sense of self as male. Their bodies become signals that they are female, seemingly betraying them. As experiences from Dante and Jameel show below, the bodily changes that arose from puberty implied a powerlessness to alter the perception that they were assigned female at birth. As Dante said:

> Well sometimes I feel like [I am a] man. I'm doing well. Honestly, most of the time I often think that I'm a dude. It is how I behave and how I think and how I act and such. And then my body just stops me from doing that because I have you know a female assigned body and such. That's the thing that confuses me.

Dante became acutely aware of his body after the onset of puberty. When Dante spoke to me, he had not come out to his family as a trans man. He lacked financial security and was unable to access any kind of procedure to alter the state of his body. He said that this restricted his ability to identify himself as a male to others. Others perceived him as a female, which made him feel worse about himself. Similarly, Jameel described his experience with puberty:

> That's when I was having this moment of not dilemma [but] confusion. Why didn't I like wearing girls' clothes when I was born a woman? And it builds up in my mind. So I got more depressed. Dysphoria sinks in and then I developed feminine features like breasts and it kind of haunts me in a way.

Jameel recalled his history of depression and recounts its first occurrence when his mother pushed him towards becoming feminine by wearing the hijab, female clothing, and make-up. He obliged his mother's requests to avoid getting into trouble with her. The development of breasts was a significant change for him, marking the onset of dysphoria. Yet, because Jameel did not yet know that he was a trans man,[19] he still could not understand why any of this was happening to him. Rubin (2003) has noted that

---

19   Jameel referred himself as a trans man when speaking about his childhood experiences and dysphoria.

trans men experience more social difficulties after puberty because their bodies change from one that is relatively ungendered to one that is female. Unlike menstruation, breasts are visible markers that trans men's bodies are physically female. It is a cultural sign of womanhood and an organ that is objectified, sexualised, and receives unwanted attention from others. It leaves trans men vulnerable to being misgendered and prevents them from living their lives as men. As Dante said, "my body stops me."

Jake described his experience of discomfort and dissonance when his body started changing during puberty. His developing breasts confused him, but he recognised that he was expected to be feminine and that his body was like that of other females. Nonetheless, he could not understand why he felt discomfort when he had to wear female attire. He described his experience with the bra:

> At that time I didn't know what LGBT[Q] was. I didn't know what transgender was. All I knew was tomboy. I don't even feel that I was a guy. I just knew that I [was] just me. This is me. Whatever you ask me to do I [will] try but if I don't like [I won't do it]. If you asked me to wear a push-up bra and I don't like it [I will] switch to a sports bra. I prefer a sports bra but it's still a bra in my head. It's just a sports bra [is] a bit more tight but that's [a] comfort. I didn't think of binding. I didn't even know there was binding. I just knew that sports bras make my breasts thinner and binds it a bit more so I can run more and that's all I thought. I can play more sports with the guys.

Like Jameel, Jake also experienced a push from his mother to be feminine. He displayed resistance by making concessions about how he expressed femininity. The "push-up bra"—an article of clothing that accentuates and sexualises female bodies—was exchanged with a sports bra. This negotiation allowed Jake to not only have freedom of movement when playing sports, but also minimised the size of his breasts. Society reads one's assigned sex based on an assessment of whether they have certain criteria; if someone has breasts, they must be female.

Men are not supposed to have breasts, but women are, highlighting the binary opposition of gendered bodies. As Iris Marion Young (2005, p. 76) put it, "In our culture that focuses to the extreme on breasts, a woman, especially in the adolescent years but also through the rest of her life, often feels herself judged and evaluated according to the size and contours of her breasts, and indeed she often is." As the most visible signs of a woman's femininity and sexuality, breasts are purported to be essential for men

GROWING UP "FEMALE"

(cis and trans) to look at and enjoy (Ward et al., 2006, p. 704). Women are often judged and evaluated on the size and shape of their breasts. There are many meanings assigned to breasts—womanhood, sexuality, shame. They are objectified and thought to belong to others—male partners, children, and people who look at them. Objectified in the media, they are used to sell products (Saltman, 1998). The only men who are allowed to have breasts are bodybuilders, where they are "massive mounds" of muscle which act to maintain gender norms and gender differences by virtue of physicality (Saltman, 1998, p. 48). Jake is not a bodybuilder, and therefore, breasts on his body are a marker of femininity and a point of sexual gazing, especially by men. For trans men, breasts are the body part that are most likely to prevent them from living full lives, as breasts inhibit them from living full time as men and cause the most discomfort when they look in the mirror (Rubin, 2003). Many trans men start breast binding at puberty, though some also choose not to because it can be physically restrictive, leading to breathing difficulties. Other trans men spoke to me of other kinds of discomfort caused by their growing breasts. Now being gazed on and judged for the visibility (or lack thereof) of their breasts, the experience compounded their cognitive dissonance, heightening their gender dysphoria. The distress arising from dysphoria is an extremely difficult experience for transgender people. Hans spoke of his experience of dysphoria during puberty:

> You know females grow certain parts. I didn't want that. So I kind of hoped that I wouldn't make it past primary [school]. And then when I got into form one[20] I hoped that I didn't have to finish school. I hoped that something would happen to me and I could just go to sleep and [not] come back again.

Just as he was coming to terms with the fact that he was assigned female at birth, Hans began to experience the onset of puberty and his body changed. The experience was painful enough for Hans that he wanted to die. Likewise, Ben experienced puberty as painful. He was a 24-year-old Chinese Malaysian who said that at the onset of puberty, "[I] started growing breasts [and] was super uncomfortable with that. In the shower I would be hitting myself to suppress the growth." Ben's realisation that he is a trans man came much later, and at puberty he could not understand why his body was changing.

---

20   First year of secondary schooling. Most Malaysians start secondary education at 13 years of age.

The self-harm he inflicted on himself is evidence of the extent of distress that he and other trans men experience upon realising that their bodies are not aligned with their gender identities.

Trans men experience cognitive dissonance when they find out that they are not male. They learn this primarily through three ways: noticing their genitalia differ from other males, being told by others that they are female, and the onset of puberty. The cognitive dissonance is coupled with facing punishment from others—family members or peers—regarding the misalignment in trans men's assigned sex and expression of masculinity. Trans men are subjected to reprimands from others or social punishment in the form of teasing and bullying, especially when their sexual attraction and desires challenge the expectation of heterosexuality based on their assigned sex, i.e. they are females and are expected to be attracted to males. The non-alignment between their bodies and gender identities results in them experiencing gender dysphoria, which marks a painful realisation that they are not, in fact, boys. The next chapter will explore how trans men experience being socialised into femininity, and the impact this has on their decision-making in becoming men.

References

Agha, S. S., Thambiah, S., & Chakraborty, K. (2019). Children's agency in accessing for spaces of play in an urban high-rise community in Malaysia. *Children's Geographies, 17*(6), 691–704. https://doi.org/10.1080/14733285.2019.1574335

Ahmed, L. (2017). The veil debate—again. In C. McCann & S. K. Kim (Eds.), *Feminist theory reader: Local and global perspective* (4th ed., pp. 335–346). Routledge.

American Psychiatric Association (APA). (2014). *Answers to your questions about transgender people, gender identity and gender expression*. APA.

Bakar, N. A., Daud, N., & Abdullah, A. H. (2015). Developing integrated pedagogical approaches in play pedagogy: Malaysian experiences. *Asian Social Sciences, 11*(4). https://doi.org/10.5539/ass.v11n4p234

Bartky, S. L. (1990). *Femininity and domination: Studies in the phenomenology of oppression*. Routledge.

Bostan, C. M. (2016). The authentic self—determinant role in attaining common goals. *Psihologia Sociala, 1*(37), 55–66.

Budgeon, S. (2003). Identity as an embodied event. *Body & Society, 9*(1), 35–55. https://doi.org/10.1177/1357034X030091003

Butler, J. (1999). *Gender trouble*. Routledge.

Festinger, L. (1957). *A theory of cognitive dissonance*. Stanford University Press.

Foucault, M. (1977). *Discipline and punish: The birth of the prison*. Random House.

Ghazali, N. (2016). Islamic education in Malaysia: Analysing the significance of appreciating the Shafi'i school. *Geografia: Malaysian Journal of Society and Space, 12*(4), 147–157.

Green, J. (2005a). Part of the package. *Men and Masculinities, 7*(3), 291–299. https://doi.org/10.1177/1097184X04272116

Halberstam, J. (1998). *Female masculinity*. Duke University Press.

Ilmi, H. S., Gheda, M. L. M. & Yusof, N. A. (2018). Neighbourhood safety and outdoor play activities among urban children in Shah Alam, Malaysia. *IOP Conf. Ser.: Mater. Sci. Eng. 401 012031*. 10.1088/1757-899X/401/1/012031

Ismail, N. A., Safiullah, S. B., Yunos, M. Y. M., Utaberta, N., & Ismail, S. (2015). Identifying natural playscape elements in a neighbourhood park: A case study of Kuantan, Malaysia. *Adv. Environ. Biol., 9*(5), 504–513.

Kernis, M. H., & Goldman, B. M. (2006). A multicomponent conceptualisation of authenticity: Theory and research. *Advances in Experimental Social Psychology, 38*, 238–357. https://doi.org/10.1016/S00065-2601(06)38006-9

Kilvington, J., & Wood, A. (2016). *Gender, sex, and children's play*. Bloomsbury Academic.

Looi, S. (2020, 14 January). Malaysian actress Liyana Jasmay lashes out against fan who offered advice on donning a hijab. *The Malay Mail*. https://www.malaymail.com/news/showbiz/2020/01/14/malaysian-actress-liyana-jasmay-lashes-out-against-fan-who-offers-advice-on/1827889

O'Neil, J., Wester, S. R., Heesacker, M., & Snowden, S. J. (2017). Masculinity as a heuristic: Gender role conflict theory, superorganisms, and system-level thinking. In R. F. Levant & Y. J. Wong (Eds.), *The psychology of men and masculinities* (pp. 75–103). American Psychological Association. https://doi.org/10.1037/0000023-004

Rizvi, S. A. H., Naqvi, S. A. A., Hussain, M., & Hasan, A. S. (1999). Religious circumcision: A Muslim view. *BJU International, 83*(Suppl. 1), 13–16. https://doi.org/10.1046/j.1464-410x.1999.083s1013.x

Robinson, J. L., & Demaree, H. A. (2007). Physiological and cognitive effects of expressive dissonance. *Brain and Cognition, 63*(1), 70–78. https://doi.org/10.1016/j.bandc.2006.08.003

Rogers, M. F. (1999). *Barbie culture*. Sage Publications.

Rubin, H. (2003). *Self-made men: Identity and embodiment among transsexual men*. Vanderbilt University Press.

Saltman, K. (1998). Men with breasts. *Journal of the Philosophy of Sport, 25*(1), 48–60. https://doi.org/10.1080/00948705.1998.9714568

Sheriff, S., Rani, W. N. W. M., & Mohamed, N. A. N. (2019). *Perceptions and realities the public and personal rights of Muslim women in Malaysia: Findings from the survey on Muslim women's realities in Malaysia*. Sisters in Islam.

Tan, M. Z. (8 May 2019). 'Dehijabing' by female celebs can have negative influence, says Perkasa's women's wing chief. *The Malay Mail.* https://www.malaymail.com/news/life/2019/05/08/dehijabing-by-female-celebs-can-have-negative-influence-says-perkasa-womens/1750843

Tan, M. Z. (12 June 2020). Malaysian singer Zizi Kirana 'stressed out' after getting bashed online for removing hijab. *The Malay Mail.* https://www.malaymail.com/news/showbiz/2020/06/12/malaysian-singer-zizi-kirana-stressed-out-after-getting-bashed-online-for-r/1874776

Ward, L. M., Merriwether, A., & Caruthers, A. (2006). Breasts are for men: Media, masculinity ideologies, and men's beliefs about women's bodies. *Sex Roles, 55.* 703–714. https://doi.org/10.1007/s11199-006-9125-9

West, C., & Zimmerman, D. H. (1987). Doing gender. *Gender & Society, 1*(2), 125–151. https://doi.org/10.1177/0891243287001002002

Yogyakarta Principles. (2006). *The Yogyakarta Principles: Principles on the application of international human rights law to sexual orientation and gender identity.* Geneva: United Nations. https://yogyakartaprinciples.org/

Yogyakarta Principles. (2017). *The Yogyakarta Principles plus 10: Additional principles and state obligations on the application of international human rights law in relation to sexual orientation, gender identity, gender expression and sex characteristics to complement the Yogyakarta Principles.* Geneva: United Nations. https://yogyakartaprinciples.org/

Young, I. M. (2005). *On female body experience: Throwing like a girl and other essays.* Oxford University.

Zurairi, A. R. (17 April 2019) 'Dehijabbing' forum panellists accuse Jais of harassing, intimidating female activists. *The Malay Mail.* https://www.malaymail.com/news/malaysia/2019/04/17/dehijabing-forum-panelists-accuse-jais-of-harassing-intimidating-female-act/1743964

3. Experiencing Femininity

Abstract: Qualitative analysis of 23 in-depth semi-structured interviews with Malaysian trans men revealed their experiences of being disciplined into femininity. Having not been socialised as boys, trans men faced and resisted strict policing of their bodies and behaviours to embody femininity. They encountered gender expectations based on ideas of femininity and their cultural backgrounds. Interviewees describe their experiences of being disciplined into femininity through controls on their appearance and movement. They also experience disciplining into femininity through violence. This chapter explores their experiences of gender-based violence, and the impact this has on their decision-making about masculinity. This experience also signifies the inevitability of female histories in their lives and future decision-making as men.

Keywords: trans men, Malaysia, cognitive dissonance, discipline, gender-based violence

Trans men faced with the contradictory information between their identity and their bodies, along with information from their environments, experience cognitive dissonance resulting in feelings of uncertainty about themselves. This experience is compounded by others denying their male identities and actively, even violently, reminding them that they are female. This chapter shows how these experiences police trans men's gender expression, discouraging their expressions of masculinity. This happened first via socialisation as female, where the trans men received subtle, and not-so-subtle, indications of behaviours expected of girls and women. They experienced restrictions on behaviour and movement, expectations to participate in beauty rituals as part of doing femininity, and cultural and religious means of enforcing femininity. I use the term "binaric complementarity" to signal the assumption that gender differences are due to the natures of men (male) and women (female), and

---

Kumaresan, Vizla. *Trans Men in Malaysia: Decision-Making, Masculinity and Manhood.* Amsterdam: Amsterdam University Press, 2025.
DOI: 10.5117/9789048562596_CH03

between men's rational and women's emotional dispositions.[1] Gender complementarity assumes that men and women possess complementary sets of strengths and weaknesses, which are stereotypes of behaviours and roles. Binaric complementarity assumes and reifies the notion that there are only two genders which are the opposite of, and opposed to, each other. The second way the trans men experienced femininity was through gender-based violence (GBV) used as a method of reminding them of their status as female. These experiences of GBV consequently influenced the trans men's decision-making processes on doing masculinity and becoming men.

Trans men's experiences of socialisation as female and GBV are largely shaped by prevalent gender norms, which are widely held societal norms and attitudes of how males and females are expected to behave (Chandra-Mouli et al., 2018, p. 239). These norms come with the notion that what is male is held to higher value compared to what is female and is a way in which societies perpetuate gender inequalities (Chandra-Mouli et al., 2018, p. 239). These values are implied when children are socialised as male or female. Theories of gender socialisation argue that gender becomes entrenched during adolescence (Chandra-Mouli et al., 2018, p. 239), but trans men's narratives demonstrate that, despite being socialised as female, they continued to identify as male and negotiated and resisted socialisation as female. Despite backlashes from their environment, they were able to challenge and question both the female and male norms that they were taught, and found ways to develop new ideas of gender that aligned with their own values and beliefs. Trans men's experiences with gender socialisation, therefore, demonstrate that it is not a passive process. Instead, it is fraught with struggles between notions of the self, and dominant social and cultural forces and power.

Learning to Be Female

The trans men experienced gendered socialisation through constant reminders of the expectations of femininity, which served to reify gender

---

1   I refer here to Ziba Mir-Hosseini's (2022) explanation of the evolution of gender equality discourse within Islamic laws and cultures. She explains (p. 26) that the concepts of "gender equity" or "gender complementarity" are used to rationalise the differences between Islamic laws and practices and the movement for gender equality. Though termed "modernist," Mir-Hosseini argues that this move is "neo-traditionalist."

EXPERIENCING FEMININITY

norms—binary constructs of masculinity and femininity. Miles's experience exemplifies this. He was 28 years old and identified as Chindian.[2] He talked to me about being told to behave like a girl:

> In school. It was cool until I was 13. Then when I started attending co-ed school then people started to tell me to behave more like a girl. They [said] if you don't grow your hair [or] if you don't start behaving like a girl you're not going to get boyfriends.

Miles only began to experience being disciplined to be feminine when he entered a mixed-sex secondary school. When discussing his gender expression when he was a child, he said he was "Okay with anything. I just [didn't] like things that are hyper-feminine." While he preferred wearing boys' clothes, he could not avoid wearing the girls' school uniform. Boys at school never said anything about his gender expression yet would treat him like a "straight female." It was the female students and teachers who would police his gender expression. He particularly recalls female students telling him to grow his hair long. The aim of behaving like a girl, he was told, was to get boys' sexual and romantic attention.

Miles experienced a form of female socialisation called appearance culture, where adolescent girls incorporate sociocultural standards for female beauty into their peer cultures (Clark & Tiggemann, 2006; Jones & Crawford, 2006). Appearance culture focuses on looking good and fitting in and has been found to relate to eating disorders and a preference for thinness among adolescent girls (Carey et al., 2010). There are three elements of appearance culture: appearance conversations—which Miles was subjected to—peer appearance criticism and teasing, and exposure to appearance-focused media. The practices of appearance culture create shared endorsement of the ideal appearance and involve continual attention to members' appearance, resulting in a culture of surveillance amongst and between adolescent females.

Alexis also experienced scrutiny about the length of his hair while in school. He was 28 years old and Malay. He had migrated abroad to seek asylum on the grounds of being discriminated against in Malaysia because he identified as transgender. He lived with his male partner. He wanted to speak to me for this study as he felt it was an important opportunity to break the silence around the experiences of trans men

---

2   A common Malaysian term to refer to someone of Chinese and Indian mixed parentage.

in Malaysia. Recalling his struggles with gender expression in school, he said:

> The biggest thing I can remember is no don't cut your hair. I always wanted short hair. Like even when I was young I wouldn't be allowed to cut my hair because you have to show your face shape or girls are supposed to have long hair. Even when I went to the hairdresser I would ask [if I can] get my hair cut short. And they'd be like no. Your face isn't right for it.

Miles and Alexis learned, through being reprimanded to behave like a girl, that masculine is that which feminine is not. Miles said: "You kind of learn the opposite is how people would expect a boy would react," thus implying that the genders are connected through a binaric complementarity. Having his hair in a certain style was a signifier of his sex—"girls are supposed to have long hair"; the "supposed to" here denotes an expectation of being natural. He learnt that beauty practices play an important role in sex differentiation. It is necessary so the sexes can be told apart; beauty practices create and represent the differences between the sexes (Jeffreys, 2014, p. 7).

Aside from hair being an indication of his assigned sex at birth, school was also where Alexis experienced disciplining for not presenting properly as female. He explained that his hair is curly with a tendency to frizz. Alexis's teachers constantly reprimanded him for not having tidy hair. Ben also had a similar experience at school: "I think they tried to get me to grow my hair. But then I did that and it was really messy and then they asked me to cut my hair short." This scrutiny that Miles, Alexis, and Ben faced for their hairstyles can be attributed to the expectation that girls and women are to always appear pleasant-looking and must invest themselves in looking pleasing to others (Bartky, 1990, p. 28). Women's commitment to beauty is also seen as an aspect that separates them from men (Jeffreys, 2014, p. 7). This commitment to beauty requires investments of time and money, as well as accepting pain and emotional distress. For Miles, Ben, and Alexis, the attitudes of others about their hair became an indication of societal expectations of their gender and expressions of femininity. It was to communicate to them the appropriate and acceptable ways of being and doing feminine. It was also a way to communicate to them that their masculine expressions needed remedying.

Trans men also encountered other kinds of behavioural expectations about gender norms. Asher was a 21-year-old Chinese Malaysian attending university abroad. He recalled how he and his brother received different treatment from their parents:

> Say like there's a birthday party that I want [to attend]. My parents would say no to me and if my brother asks the same thing my parents would [consent]. Because [he is] a guy and [he] can. And then my parents would constantly [tell me] you're a girl and people will take advantage of you. My parents are more supportive [of] my brother. [They] want him to go into more sports but when it comes to me [playing] basketball my parents [ask me to] go for less sporty things like drawing or things like that.

Social and movement restrictions are common forms of disciplining for girl children. Asher recognised that this was "absurd" and did not understand the rationale for it. His parents explained that they wanted to protect him from being exploited by others; they perceived that being female made him vulnerable to exploitation. Aside from playing sports, Asher's brother was also encouraged to "Go and dream" and do whatever he wanted. Asher, on the other hand, was used to hearing "No, you can't" when he wanted to play sports. He was also expected to sit and behave in certain ways due to being assigned female.

According to the United Nations International Children's Fund (UNICEF, 2019.), children face different risks for different forms of violation of rights determined by gender, poverty, and social norms, amongst other factors. The Counter-Trafficking Data Collaborative (CTDC, 2017) reports that girl children face a higher risk of sexual exploitation, as evidence from international trafficking of humans indicates. Many families, thus, justify the need to place more restrictions on girl children to control for this vulnerability. Asher's parents view him as at risk of being sexually exploited due to him being assigned female.

Gender norms which are produced by patriarchal power relations also play a role in the imposition of these restrictions (Bankar et al., 2018). These social restrictions have real-life outcomes for women and girls. In India, for example, gender norms play a more important role than economic factors in determining a woman's age of marriage (Bankar et al., 2018). Restricting girls' access to public spaces also has consequences for girls' access to education and participation in the public sphere as citizens. While limiting women's and girl children's access to public spaces is meant to protect them from sexual violence, such moves maintain male privilege at the expense of women's freedom of movement (Bankar et al., 2018). Asher's frustrations about these restrictions arise due to him identifying as male, and not having the freedom to do the things he wanted. The restrictions denied his agency by limiting the opportunity and ability, which were available to his brother, to decide for himself.

Dante also experienced impositions of restrictions. He said his parents treated him differently from his brother because he was assigned female. Like Asher, Dante faced restrictions on his movements, which his brothers did not face. His brothers also seemed to have a free hand in making decisions for themselves, such as the ability to "go out whenever they want." Dante's brothers are open about their relationships with their girlfriends with encouragement from their parents. He and his sister had to take on the responsibility of helping with household chores. Like his sister, Dante was encouraged to have a boyfriend. His parents also forced him to wear the hijab and *baju kurung*.[3] Dante resisted his parents' encouragement for him to have feminine gender expression.

UNICEF reports that girl children are far more likely than boys to do housework and this can sometimes impact their access to education. While Dante did not experience such an impact, for him it was the imposition of a gender norm geared towards shaping his gender identity as female and feminine. Labour is one of the ways in which gender expression is supposedly evident. The doing of labour—men's work and women's work—differentiates the masculine (male) and the feminine (female) (West & Zimmerman, 1987, p. 128). In this case, Dante engaging in housework is an example of him doing gender, that gender being female, despite him identifying as male. Dante was forced to constantly and routinely enact these behaviours to sustain the feminine identity for himself and others. It functions as a means for everyone to know their place or role in interactions. Any person engaging in the behaviours of the other category disrupts the arrangement.

The reminder to "behave like a girl" acts as a powerful tool for disciplining trans men's gender identity and expression. Jakc told me:

> Definitely my parents were the very first ones to keep telling me you have got to behave like a girl. The neighbours, my teachers [and] even my friends will tell me you are not behaving like a girl. You're wearing a pinafore[4] but you got the pants underneath. The pants are there so you can sit a bit more *kangkang*[5] but you're not supposed to take off your pinafore and run around with the pants and a white shirt which is what

3   A long-sleeved and loose-fitting tunic worn with a long skirt.
4   Girls' school uniform.
5   Malay for sitting with legs spread wide.

EXPERIENCING FEMININITY

> I did. A lot of people [were telling me off]. Nearly everyone I remember was telling me why don't you just be a bit more girly? Sit correctly. Eat properly. Dress up a bit better.

Jake was reprimanded every time his behaviours were deemed unfeminine. Like Alexis, Jake was never told what "girl" behaviours were. He simply knew that he was doing it wrong. As far as Jake was concerned, he only did that which came naturally to him. "Behave like a girl" is a form of social constraint which comprises asset distributions, rules, norms, and preferences that afford more freedom, opportunities, and benefits for some and not others (Young, 2005, p. 21). Some of these constraints are defined through the law, and others through cultural norms. There are consequences to not conforming to them. In Jake's and Asher's experiences, these rules encompassed sitting, eating, and dressing up "correctly," "properly," and "better." Their price for not conforming was constant surveillance, disciplining, and being denied opportunities to do what they wanted. Asher, Dante, and Jake's families and peers assumed that being assigned female makes them feminine; that femininity is a natural consequence of the state of being female. Their competency to perform femaleness and femininity is thus expected—that they must possess the know-how without being taught. Aside from the assumption that these behaviours should come naturally from being assigned female, it was also expected that these behaviours are known, as they are prevalent in culture and passed down through tradition.

The Force of Culture and Tradition

It was primarily the Malay and/or Muslim trans men who spoke to me about socialisation into femininity through culture and tradition. Mitch was 52 years old, an NGO worker, and identified as Malay. He is Muslim and referred to his partner as his wife. Together, they raise two children. He told me about his mother's reaction to his displays of masculine behaviour when he was a teenager:

> So the news about me going around as a lesbian was hot at that point in time. [My mom said] to me you have to be more like a girl *supaya orang tak cakap macam*[6] don't talk about this to you and all that. And I said

---

6   So people don't talk about you.

yeah but I don't know how to behave like a girl. How does a girl behave? *Cuba pakai skirt. Cuba pakai baju kurung.*[7] But I don't like to wear all that because that's not me.

Mitch explained that rumours of him being a lesbian were an issue at his school; he had experienced being disciplined for exhibiting close relationships with women. Mitch realised much later in adulthood that he was a trans man. When he was younger, he first identified as a lesbian and then later as *pengkid*.[8] At school, Mitch challenged his religious teachers' views on lesbians and was disciplined for that, too. His mother thought that getting him to behave in feminine ways, i.e. wearing skirts or the *baju kurung*, would prevent people from talking about him and calling him lesbian. For her, it was important that people did not gossip about him.

In Mitch's case there was an expectation on him to cultivate a good reputation in the community. Girls and women are expected to be custodians of family honour and have a responsibility to avoid any kind of public censure that will taint their reputation (Bankar et al., 2018). Honour serves to regulate public conduct to police group boundaries (Gorringe, 2016). How one conducts oneself in public is meant to signal in-groups and out-groups. However, the lines between public and private are blurred, for example, with sexual behaviours or preferences. Cultural norms are, hence, used to regulate private lives, and this is evident in how Mitch's mother wanted him to behave in accordance with cultural expectations of femininity, i.e. to wear skirts or the *baju kurung*. There is a gender difference when it comes to honour, where women embody a group's honour, whereas men possess it (Gorringe, 2016, p. 259). Hence, men are required to enforce honour amongst women in the group. When men act dishonourably, they risk shaming themselves, while women's actions affect the standing of the community (Gorringe, 2016, p. 259). Therefore, it is incumbent that women's behaviours are always scrutinised. It is not unusual that it was Mitch's mother who enforced these expectations on him, as in Malay communities it is the role of women to maintain kin and neighbourly relations (Ong, 1995, p. 141).

Mitch's experiences of coming to terms with his identity required him to navigate not only Malay cultural expectations of femininity but also sexuality. He began to identify as a *pengkid* at this time. *Pengkid* has become a localised term for a masculine-looking Malay and Muslim lesbian (Wong,

---

7   Try wearing a skirt. Try wearing a *baju kurung.*
8   Masculine looking Malay-Muslim lesbian.

EXPERIENCING FEMININITY

2012) and has often been conflated with tomboys or masculine-looking lesbian women. Coupled with the state's clamping down on and punishing transgressions of heteronormative ideals, spaces for Malay-Muslim women to express non-heterosexual identities are limited and dangerous. Identifying as *pengkid* allows many girls and young women to enjoy the freedom and social space to transgress the prevailing normative (feminine and heterosexual) gender expectations that are likely imposed onto their female sex and bodies (Wong, 2012). Through the adoption of a more masculine gender expression, Malay-Muslim females are able to resist the restrictions and gender expectations imposed on them. Hans spoke about the expectations placed on him as a Malay Muslim female:

> I woke up late, like 10am. So [my father came] up to my room to wake me up. [He said] stuff like *kamu tu anak dara bangun la awal sikit*.[9] Like what does that even mean? Does it mean boys can sleep in? Girls can't do that?

Hans recalled that his father was more likely to treat him differently because he was not a boy. He spoke with sadness at the memory of not being taken to a car exhibition with his brothers because his father said, "Only boys should do things like that." Aside from expecting him to be up early because he was *anak dara*,[10] his father would call on Hans to help his mother with the chores. Hans became annoyed at this, and he asked his father why he was not helping and why his brothers were not being called to help. His father then slapped him.

Hans's father policing his behaviour is an example of the gender bias inherent in Malay cultural norms. Morality—expectations of virginity and maintaining a good reputation—are methods of gender differentiation in Malay culture. A man's role is one of guardianship—of his sisters', wives' (as a Muslim man is allowed up to four wives under polygamy laws in Malaysia), and daughters' virtue (Ong, 1995, p. 140). Therefore, Hans's father's expectations of him as an *anak dara* was the former performing his role as the patriarchal head of his household. Islamic expectations of female chastity impose more rigorous restrictions on unmarried women, the *anak dara*. The *anak dara* is expected to be "bashful and modest" (Ong, 1995, p. 140). A man's identity, according to Islamic law, is defined in terms of preparing his son(s) for running his own household and controlling the sexuality of his wife and daughter(s) (Ong, 1995, p. 141). Hans's challenging

9   Malay for, "You are a virgin girl, and you should wake up early."
10   Virgin girl.

of his father is usually unacceptable, resulting in him being slapped. Like Hans, the trans men came to recognise that challenging expectations of gender expression and identity could result in violence.

The Force of Violence

Violence is used to enforce femininity in various ways. Mitch experienced social censure in the form of gossiping. Hans experienced physical violence when his father slapped him for his supposed transgression. Damon experienced another kind of violence from his own father. About his father, Damon said:

> He is pretty weird. He would say, you know if you wear [really] short skirts then people will see your panties. Like how are people supposed to know [you are female]? Because you don't have breasts. And, I would be like what? What?

Damon's father controlled how Damon dressed in order for him to perform a certain kind of femininity. Where previously he wanted Damon dressed in pink, here he wanted Damon dressed in a short skirt so that glimpses of his panties would enable others to read him as female since his breasts were not obvious. Damon would typically resist his father's efforts to coerce him to dress in skirts and dresses but would eventually have to comply. He recalled one incident where he put on his sister's dress, which had a zipper in the front; Damon had pulled the zipper all the way up to the nape of his neck. When in public, Damon's father reached out and pulled the zipper down to reveal his cleavage despite Damon's attempts to pull it back up.

Damon's father highlighting to him that his breasts were not obvious reifies societal expectations on bodies to convey a person's sex. By pulling down the zipper to reveal his breasts, Damon's father is also sexually harassing him and rendering him powerless over his own body in that social situation. Revealing Damon's breasts was an act of sexualising and objectifying him, thus reminding him of the expectations of him as a female to not only be feminine but also visibly so, and that his body is a sexual one meant for the pleasures of others.

The incident followed an earlier encounter where Damon was forced to change out of his masculine-style clothing to wear his sister's dress. His father expressed disapproval of Damon's masculine dressing by giving Damon's mother a look which he knew to interpret with fear and apprehension. The series of events reminded him of his inferior position in his family. As a girl child, Damon was subjected to the realities of life as a female person and learnt the powerlessness that is a form of oppression that women become subjected to. This powerlessness threatens women's autonomy and self-determination (Bartky, 1990). While Damon did not identify as female, his father subjected him to the same kind of treatment he meted out to his mother and sisters; his father beat him and frequently threatened him with physical violence. Damon lived in constant fear of his father. The effect is to render the (female) person powerless and subject to male power, demonstrated in the form of violence. This powerlessness to violence would come to inform Damon's later decision-making on masculinity.

Trans men experience femininity being enforced on them in the form of expectations of their appearance, where their engagement in beauty rituals means to separate them from males. Their childhood experiences of learning the binaric complementarity of gender are reinforced through the heterosexual expectation that they are to perform femininity in order to be attractive to males. They also experience femininity through restrictions on their movement. Malay-Muslim trans men further experience femininity within the context of their culture, which carries with it the implications of chastity and honour. Their experience of violence is a reminder of their powerlessness within a male-dominated society and continues through experiences of gender-based violence.

Experiences of Gender-Based Violence

The socialisation into femininity that the trans men endured demonstrated that the process relies on reifying and affirming gender stereotypes. The process perpetuates patriarchal power structures which position women and girls lower than men and boys. Social policing is a tool for disciplining people into conforming to gender normativity. Violence is a powerful tool used to keep people in line and maintain power relations and structures through the perpetuation of gender norms. Gender-based violence is another tool that maintains those gendered power structures. The European Commission (n.d.) defines GBV as "violence directed against a person because of that person's gender or violence that affects a person of a particular gender disproportionately" and includes physical, sexual, and physical violence. The United Nations Population Fund (UNFPA) (n.d.) states that GBV is disproportionately prevalent among women.

Recognising women's increased vulnerability to GBV, the Committee on the Elimination of All forms of Discrimination against Women (CEDAW) (2017), in its general recommendation 35, uses the term "gender-based violence against women" to highlight the "gendered causes and impacts of the violence," and goes on to state that "gender-based violence against women is one of the fundamental social, political and economic means by which the subordinate position of women with respect to men and their stereotyped roles are perpetuated." Thus, prevalent male gender norms are implicated in the perpetration and perpetuation of GBV. However, men are also victims of GBV. The Institute for Security Studies (ISS) reports that cultural stereotypes about men play a role in the perpetuation of GBV against men. Men are more likely to report incidents of sexual violence they have witnessed and not what they have experienced because acts perpetrated in GBV against men are seen as emasculating and, also, due to destructive cultural stereotypes where men are viewed as sexually dominant and women as submissive (Ngari, 2016).

Violence experienced by transgender people is also a form of GBV; they are targeted for violence because of their gender. The contexts in which transgender people live increase their vulnerability to GBV across their lifespans, and they risk GBV during the stages of gender identity formation, transition, and expression (Dominguez-Martinez et al., 2020). The experiences of GBV documented here show that they act to remind trans men of their status as female, and come to influence later decision-making about masculinity.

Reminders of the Status of Female

John was a 21-year-old Indian Malaysian working in media. Speaking about accessing public spaces with cisgender men, he said:

> I'm afraid. If they know me [or] if [it's] my best friend I have no problem. If [it's] other men I will be afraid. Because in public transport [cis men] sees [me] as a girl. They [will] come [close to me and touch my] private parts. I have faced [problems] like that.

John had not yet started his medical transitioning but was socially transitioning. He dressed in men's clothes and used male pronouns. He had come out as a trans man to his family, friends, and colleagues, who all affirmed his identity. His girlfriend regards him as a man, and they plan to marry.

EXPERIENCING FEMININITY

While people close to him treat him like a man, others continue to perceive him as female and misgender him. For John, the worst experience of being misgendered was sexual harassment. He experienced it especially when he used public transport, which made him fearful. The fear was so pervasive for John that he thought about it even when he was not in situations where he would encounter sexual harassment. He lives in a state of sexual terrorism (Sheffield, 1987) where sexual harassment is an everyday practice that creates and perpetuates the state of fear (Kissling, 1991). The end goal is social control, which enforces special boundaries where women are seen as trespassers in public spaces that belong to men.

John and other trans men are not women. But being assigned female at birth, and with John being visible as female, he and other trans men are subject to the sexual harassment that women experience. These incidents are reminders to trans men like John that they are perceived as female and that their status as women subject them to evaluation as sexual objects in ways that men are not (Kissling, 1991). As John experienced, being touched in the chest or genital area reminds people assigned female of their vulnerability to these and other violations, and that they are seldom, if ever, in a position to treat men this way. For John and other trans men, the vulnerability is at least twofold due to their status as transgender people in an environment that does not offer them any legal or social protection.

These experiences of GBV happen in families, too, as Jervind described. He was a 33-year-old Chinese Malaysian employed in the finance industry. He remembered waking up one night when he was a teenager because he felt someone touching him:

> I [was] very scared because my brother sometimes harassed me and my sister. I [could not be] sure whether [that was my] imagination or [real] because [I always felt someone touching me] when I slept. But then I [would] open my eyes [and there would be] no one. But I [would] see the *bayang*.[11] [Once I heard] a sound and it was my brother. I don't know what he [was] doing that time. Then one day my sister shouted so I rushed to my sister and I saw him run out from the room. So I confirmed [it was] him.

When Jervind reported the incident to his mother, she told him, "It's ok. All guys [are] like that." It was something that Jervind said he "couldn't accept so I hated my body more." This conversation with his mother led Jervind to bind his breasts "[M]ore. Even at night. It was painful." At the time, Jervind

11 Malay for shadow.

had not yet learnt about chest binders, so he used masking tape for binding. He recalled that he would bleed every time he removed the tape in the shower. Like John, he was perpetually gripped by fear; "I [was] very scared," he says. Jervind learnt from his mother's response that he cannot fight his brother and must accept what happened to him because she believes that "guys are like that." Attitudes such as this have been shown to contribute to the perpetuation of GBV; traditional views about gender and sexuality are factors that contribute to an environment of permissiveness for GBV (Sinacore et al., 2017, p. 10).

There were other ways trans men encountered GBV as reminders of their status as female. LaudeB described his experience with boys at his school when he was an adolescent:

> I was always looked down on because I liked girls. But then again I was always booed at or made fun of because [men] thought I was a lesbian. I have got [men] threatening me that they will make me straight again by having sex with me and all that. Most of these fellas did that because the girl that they liked was giving me attention.

Like White Lotus and Dines, LaudeB was also teased for being sexually attracted to women; others' assumption was that LaudeB was lesbian because he was read as female. Aside from the teasing, men would also threaten to "have sex" with him to correct his sexuality so he would be a "straight" woman, i.e. attracted to men. LaudeB experienced these threats, especially when men perceived him as a threat or competition for the attention of women. The threat of rape, here, was used as a form of social punishment as a means of exerting discipline on gender identity, expression, or sexuality that challenge the assumption of heterosexuality. Though it is unclear if the boys would have gone through with the threat, LaudeB still lives in a state of fear about his gender identity.

According to the United Nations (UN) Office of the High Commission for Human Rights (OHCHR, n.d.):

> Gender-based crimes of violence are a result of rampant cultural misogyny, frequently and wrongly justified or tolerated in the name of tradition, culture or religion. The sexual violence and mental torment to which girls and women are subjected both in private and public settings reinforce the subordinate status of women and give expression to patriarchal control over women's bodies and sexuality.

Rape, and the threat of rape, are results of a culture in which women's position in society is lower than men's. Rape is also a means of reinforcing women's lower status in society. Furthermore, the OHCHR, in its 2008 resolution 1820 on women and peace and security, states that rape is used to "humiliate, dominate and instil fear" amongst women, girls, and communities. The OHCHR considers rape a crime against humanity. The Asian-Pacific Resource and Research Centre for Women (ARROW) state that rape is not about sex but is about power and sexual violence. Corrective rape is a specific kind of gender-based violence perpetrated on females to punish and "cure" women of their sexual orientation (ActionAid, 2009). In documenting testimonies of women subjected to "corrective rape," ActionAid (2009) reports that verbal abuse before and during the rape focused on being "taught a lesson" and being "shown how to be real women and what a real man tasted like." The rape is a form of punishment for daring to step outside the boundaries of what their families, communities, and wider society prescribe for women (ActionAid, 2009). Corrective rape has been recognised as a weapon of hate used to discipline sexuality (Morrissey, 2013, p. 78). In LaudeB's case, the threat of rape was to punish him for taking away the attention of females coveted by the other boys. He needed to be reminded of his place as a female and that the attentions of females are meant only for those boys.

A chilling aspect of LaudeB's telling of this incident is the nonchalant way that the boys made the threat to him. LaudeB reflected on it, thinking they did not display any remorse for making the threat. Accounts of such incidences attribute it to the fact that violence in the service of upholding valuable cultural norms such as heterosexuality is not something about which to be ashamed (Morrissey, 2013). Furthermore, the boys would have perceived this threat as acceptable as they did not fear reprisal for their actions. This lack of fear on their part may be due to them believing that they were doing the right thing because corrective rape can be validated if it supports a widely accepted cultural logic (Morrissey, 2013), which in this case is heterosexuality and the dominant position of men. It is also worth noting that LaudeB's telling of the incident denoted an unexpected casualness. It was as if he had normalised this threat of rape as a way men perform masculinity to establish their power and dominance over others, especially females. All these experiences of GBV inevitably impact trans men's perception of masculinity and their later decision-making about their own masculinity and manhood.

Influences on Decision-Making

Trans men's experiences with GBV come to play a role in their decision-making processes regarding masculinity. LaudeB's experience indicated to him how he should not behave as a man. Similarly, others spoke of their experiences of GBV and the influence it had on them as men. Alexis explained how his experiences of sexual harassment affected how he now behaves with women:

> Definitely a lot more careful about how I conduct myself around women because I know I'm not one of them. I don't want to cross boundaries because I know a lot of men who do. And like having first-hand experience with that I don't want to be one of those guys who kind of don't know when to stop being too familiar with women or like [being] too handsy with women.

Alexis spoke of having experiences of sexual harassment before he transitioned. When he was younger, he faced streetside sexual harassment where men wolf-whistled or catcalled him while he was out jogging in his neighbourhood. Aside from having this kind of first-hand experience with sexual harassment, Alexis recalled hearing women talk about their experiences with sexual harassment or unwanted sexual attention and/or physical touch from men. He used these experiences to guide his behaviour with women, where his priority is for them to feel safe with and around him. Ben, too, spoke of the same kind of experience. He said he would not engage in sexually harassing behaviours that other men do when hanging out with women, "because it makes girls uncomfortable and scared and no don't do that."

Alexis and Ben have experienced sexual harassment, and sexual harassment is a form of sexual violence against women. Alexis and Ben experienced sexual harassment because they were perceived as female. Feminists argue that this is due to women being objectified; women's bodies become locations for sexual violence and women are treated as things that can be used and abused by others rather than as fellow human beings (Gervais, 2016, p. 226). When men sexually harass women or become sexually aggressive, it has less to do with the woman's thoughts, feelings, desires, and consent and is more concerned with his own uses for her, such as his own sexual fulfilment, feelings of dominance, or display of masculinity (Gervais, 2016, p. 226).

There seems to be a confirmed link between men's cognitive styles and their proclivity to sexually harass; men who have automatic cognitive associations linking sex and power show tendencies to sexually harass women (Gervais, 2016, p. 232). Power, and the need to feel it, also plays a significant role in men perpetrating non-consensual sexual behaviours towards women. Finally, the objectification of women—the perception that they are less human, likened to animals, have less agency, and are perceived as less competent—contributes to thought processes that rationalise sexual harassment.

By rejecting attitudes or behaviours that make women uncomfortable or that can be considered sexually harassing, Alexis and Ben are, firstly, refusing to objectify women. They are choosing to see women as human beings who have thoughts, feelings, and desires of their own and can consent to their participation in sexual or romantic engagements. Furthermore, because of their personal experiences with sexual harassment, they are able to challenge cognitive associations linking sex and power. This was evident in the way Alexis talked about not getting attention from women he is attracted to. Alexis identified as bisexual and was attracted to males and females. When he faced rejection from women, he perceived it as them stating their preference and not as a rejection of him as a person. He does not see it as a power struggle and can understand the woman's perspective.

Witnessing GBV also had an influence on trans men's decisions about masculinity. Kyle spoke of the domestic violence in his home when he was growing up: "My dad is very abusive. [He] neglected my mom a lot. I've seen her cry, being beaten up. [These are] also reasons why I am so protective towards girls." Kyle spoke strongly of the influence his father had on him and how he did not want to be like him. While Kyle also experienced being hit by his father, witnessing his mother's abuse played a significant role in his views of masculinity. He spoke of his struggle to manage his anger issues and his fear that he may be repeating his father's behaviours. He was steadfast about how he dealt with anger in his romantic relationships to ensure he never lashed out at his girlfriend. However, while he challenged the link between masculinity and violence, he did espouse beliefs in more traditional ideas of masculinity, such as being protective of women.

Like Alexis and Ben, Kyle perceived his father's violence from the other's perspective. Evidence indicates that perspective taking has an impact on people's reaction to social injustice. Perspective taking is a cognitive process whereby a person can adopt another person's point of view and/ or understand their psychological reactions to events. It induces a sense of psychological connectedness between the person and the target of perspective taking (Li & Edwards, 2020). People who are able to take the perspective of another identify more strongly with that person or that person's group;

and this kind of connectedness and identification is linked to an increase in sensitivity to social injustice and empathy. Alexis, Ben, and Kyle were more aware of women's sense of safety because they were able to perceive situations from their perspective.

Kyle had strong opinions on the kind of man he did not want to be, as did Cunie. He was 38 years old and self-employed. He is Malay and has a partner whom he referred to as his wife. His wife's two adopted children regarded him as their father. He said:

> I [didn't] have a good role model. I came from [a] broken marriage. I saw my father hit my mother. But he is a good father. He is a good father to [my] siblings. It's just that his marriage with my mother [was] not a good one. They always [fought]. They are divorced already. So I always think like I don't want to be like my father. I want to be a good husband. I want to be a good man. Better than my father. Provide for the family. Not just in education. Must love my wife.

Like Kyle's father, Cunie's perpetrated physical abuse on his mother. This experience influenced his views on masculinity. Cunie said he did not want to be like his father; he wanted to be a good father and husband who not only provides financially for his family but also provides love. For him, loving his wife means making sure she feels safe and can live the kind of life that she wants. Cunie grew up with financial security, but he was always worried about his parents fighting. He also spoke of not having had a close relationship with his father. His idea of masculinity encompassed one where he could be the kind of father whom his children could feel comfortable and safe approaching to talk about their problems.

Cunie and Kyle both empathised with their mothers' experiences of domestic violence. Like Kyle, taking the perspective of his mother also shaped Cunie's view of masculinity and expectations of himself as a man. However, unlike Kyle, Cunie experienced conflict because, while he believed his father was wrong in hitting his mother, he also thought that he was a "good father." Unable to reconcile the two, Cunie rationalised the domestic violence his mother experienced as an outcome of a bad marriage rather than a systemic problem arising from devaluing women's status in society. Cunie found solace for his cognitive dissonance by refusing to recognise how patriarchal gender norms contributed to the domestic violence his mother endured against his experience of having a good father.

It is not uncommon that when faced with problems with the status quo, people justify the oppressive systems that create the problems. They rationalise the status quo by falling back on stereotypes or victim-blaming (Jost & Banaji, 1994). Kyle, on the other hand, located the problem with his father and not with his parents' marriage. Cunie formed the heuristics that a man is "father and husband" as a means of helping him deal with his internal conflict. This kind of heuristic, a mental shortcut, reduces cognitive load and increases the speed of decision-making. Heuristics also help individuals perceive, comprehend, and interpret the world around them, especially in situations in which they are required to infer additional details of content, context, or meaning in specific situations (O' Neil et al., 2015). Cunie's use of these heuristics is meant as a mode of problem solving. It served a palliative function by helping resolve a conflict in Cunie's understanding of his father. Since it results in a pleasant outcome, the stereotype associated with the heuristic is strengthened.

The trans men's experiences of GBV were due to them being assigned and perceived as female, which impacted them in two ways. First, GBV was a reminder of trans men's status as female, positioning them in society as having less power than men. This relationship to power, in relation to other men, impacts how they later see themselves as men and perform masculinity. The second way that GBV impacts trans men is its role in the decision-making processes they utilise in becoming men. For some trans men, it served as a model for them of what not to emulate. For others, like Cunie, it made them believe more firmly in certain ideas of masculinity.

Part 1 of this book, chapters 2 and 3, demonstrated how trans men experienced the expression of their male gender as an example of being authentic to themselves, resulting in cognitive dissonance upon receiving information that they are not male. This cognitive dissonance became the starting point of their future decision-making processes, where their experiences as female grant them the capacity to take perspectives which influence their journeys as they transition to become men. The next chapter will explore the first part of this journey, where trans men begin to claim for themselves that they are, indeed, men.

References

ActionAid. (2009). *Hate crimes: The rise of "corrective rape" in South Africa.* UK: ActionAid.

Bankar, S., Collumbien, M., Das, M., Verma, R. K., Cislaghi, B., & Heise, L. (2018). Contesting restrictive mobility norms among female mentors implementing a sport based program for young girls in a Mumbai slum. *BMC Public Health 18*(1), 1–11. https://doi.org/10.1186/s12889-018-5347-3

Bartky, S. L. (1990). *Femininity and domination: Studies in the phenomenology of oppression*. Routledge.

Carey, R. N., Donaghue, N., & Broderick, P. (2010). 'What you look like is such a big factor': Girls' own reflections about the appearance culture in an all-girls' school. *Feminism & Psychology, 21*(3), 299–316. https://doi.org/10.1177/0959353510369893

Chandra-Mouli, V., Plesons, M., & Amin, A. (2018). Addressing harmful and unequal gender norms in early adolescence. *Nature Human Behaviour, 2*(4), 239–240. https://doi.org/10.1038/s41562-018-0318-3

Clark, L., & Tiggeman, M. (2006). Appearance culture in nine- to 12-year-old girls: Media and peer influences on body dissatisfaction. *Social Development, 15*(4), 628–643. https://doi.org/10.1111/j.1467-9507.2006.00361.x

Committee on the Elimination of Discrimination against Women (CEDAW). (2017). *General Recommendation No. 35 (2017) on gender-based violence against women, updating general recommendation No. 19*. OHCHR. https://www.ohchr.org/en/documents/general-comments-and-recommendations/general-recommendation-no-35-2017-gender-based

Counter-Trafficking Data Collaborative. (2017). *Data Stories*. CTDC. https://www.ctdatacollaborative.org/page/data-stories

Dominguez-Martinez, T., Rebeca, R. G., Fresan, A., Cruz., J., Vega, H., & Reed, G. M. (2020). Risk factors for violence in transgender people: A retrospective study of experiences during adolescence. *Psychology and Sexuality*, 1–17. https://doi.org/10.1080/19419899.2020.1802772

European Commission (n.d.) *What is Gender-Based Violence?* European Commission. https://commission.europa.eu/strategy-and-policy/policies/justice-and-fundamental-rights/gender-equality/gender-based-violence/what-gender-based-violence_fr#:~:text=gender%2Dbased%20violence-,Gender%2Dbased%20violence%20(GBV)%20by%20definition,or%20suffering%20to%20women.

Gervais, S. J. (2016). A social interaction approach to objectification: Implications for the social-psychological study of violence. In A. G. Miller (Ed.), *The social psychology of good and evil* (2nd ed., pp. 224–246). Guilford Press.

Gorringe, H. (2017). Questions of honour: Dalit women activists and the rumour mill in Tamil Nadu. *Contemporary South Asia, 25*(3), 255–269. https://doi.org/10.1080/09584935.2016.1238874

Jeffreys, S. (2014). *Beauty and misogyny: Harmful cultural practices in the West*. Routledge.

Jones, D. C., & Crawford, J. K. (2006). The peer appearance culture during adolescence: Gender and body mass variations. *Journal of Youth and Adolescence, 35*(2), 243–255. https://doi.org/10.1007/s10964-005-9006-5

Jost, J. T., & Banaji, M. R. (1994). The role of stereotyping in system-justification and the production of false consciousness. *British Journal of Social Psychology, 33*, 1–27. https://doi.org/10.1111/j.2044-8309.1994.tb01008.x

Kissling, E. A. (1991). Street harassment: The language of sexual terrorism. *Discourse on Society, 2*(4), 451–460. https://doi.org/10.1177/0957926591002004006

Li, Z., & Edwards, J. A. (2020). The relationship between system justification and perspective-taking and empathy. *Personality and Social Psychology Bulletin, 47*(1), 106–117. https://doi.org/10.1177/0146167220921041

Mir-Hosseini, Z. (2022). *Journeys toward gender equality in Islam*. Oneworld Academic.

Morrissey, M. (2013). Rape as a weapon of hate: Discursive constructions and material consequences of black lesbianism in South Africa. *Women's Studies in Communication, 36*(1), 72–91. https://doi.org/10.1080/07491409.2013.755450

Ngari, A. (2016). *Stigma, shame and destroyed livelihoods are the repercussions of sexual violence against boys and men in conflict situations*. Institute for Security Studies. https://issafrica.org/iss-today/male-victims-of-sexual-violence-wars-silent-sufferers

O'Neil, J., Wester, S. R., Heesacker, M., & Snowden, S. J. (2017). Masculinity as a heuristic: Gender role conflict theory, superorganisms, and system-level thinking. In R. F. Levant & Y. J. Wong (Eds.), *The psychology of men and masculinities* (pp. 75–103). American Psychological Association. https://doi.org/10.1037/0000023-004

Office for the High Commissioner of Human Rights (OHCHR). (n.d.). *Gender-based Violence against Women and Girls*. OHCHR. https://www.ohchr.org/en/women/gender-based-violence-against-women-and-girls

Office for the High Commissioner of Human Rights (OHCHR). (2008). *United Nations Security Council Resolution 1820, S/RES/1820*. United Nations. https://www.un.org/shestandsforpeace/content/united-nations-security-council-resolution-1820-2008-sres18202008#:~:text=%2F1820(2008)-,United%20Nations%20Security%20Council%20Resolution%201820%20(2008)%2C%20S%2F,the%20need%20for%20the%20exclusion

Ong, A. (1995). State versus Islam: Malay families, women's bodies and the body politic in Malaysia. In A. Ong & M. G. Peletz (Eds.), *Bewitching women, pious men: Gender and body politics in Asia* (pp. 159–194). University of California Press.

Sheffield, C. J. (1987). Sexual terrorism: The social control of women. In B. Hess & M. M. Ferree (Eds.), *Analysing gender: A handbook of social science research*. Sage. 171-189.

Sinacore, A. L., Durrani, S., & Khayutin, S. (2017). Men's reflections on their experiences of gender-based violence. *Journal of Interpersonal Violence, 36*(3-4), 1660–1681. https://doi.org/10.1177/0886260517742148

United Nations Chidren's Fund (UNICEF). (2019). *For Every Child, Every Right: The Convention for the Rights of the Child at a crossroads*. UNICEF.

United Nations Population Fund (UNFPA). (n.d.). *Gender-based Violence*. UNFPA. https://www.unfpa.org/gender-based-violence

West, C., & Zimmerman, D. H. (1987). Doing gender. *Gender & Society, 1*(2), 125–151. https://doi.org/10.1177/0891243287001002002

Wong, Y. (2012). Islam, sexuality and the marginal positioning of *pengkids* and their girlfriends in Malaysia. *Journal of Lesbian Studies, 16*(4), 435–448. https://doi.org/10.1080/10894160.2012.681267

Young, I. M. (2005). *On female body experience: Throwing like a girl and other essays*. Oxford University.

Part 2

I Am a Man, I Guess?

4.   Realising Male Identity

Abstract: In enquiring how trans men in Malaysia make decisions about the kind(s) of masculinity they want to express, this chapter explores how they proclaim their male identities and perform masculinity in order to be accepted by other men. In being socialised into masculinity they experience cognitive dissonance arising from conflict between masculinity heuristics—i.e. that men are sexually aggressive alongside their own experiences of facing gender-based violence when they presented as female. This chapter explores their decision-making in resolving those conflicts.

Keywords: trans men, Malaysia, decision-making, cognitive dissonance, masculinity heuristics

Cognitive dissonance is one part of the process of gender identity decision-making that trans men need to resolve. The experience of cognitive dissonance comes not only in needing to resolve the discrepancies between their perceptions of themselves as male contending with the world telling them they are female but also in recognising the unfairness of the treatment meted out on them because they were assigned female at birth. Resolving this cognitive dissonance results in them beginning to identify and live as men, a process which requires them to not only come out but pass as men.

Coming out is a process which many queer people embark on when disclosing information about their sexual orientation, gender identity, and/ or expression. The process is not only about them disclosing that information to others, but also acknowledging it to themselves (Vanderburgh, 2014). Transgender people experience coming out in terms of both gender identity/expression and sexual orientation, a process often termed transitioning. Medical transitioning involves transgender people engaging in medical procedures that result in physical changes that affirm their gender identity. Social transitioning—changing gender expression or name, for

---

Kumaresan, Vizla. *Trans Men in Malaysia: Decision-Making, Masculinity and Manhood.* Amsterdam: Amsterdam University Press, 2025.
DOI: 10.5117/9789048562596_CH04

example—presents highly visible signs of their transitioning from the sex they were assigned at birth.

Managing the elements in the personal and the public poses for transgender people the challenge of fitting in or not standing out (Vanderburgh, 2014). It requires the navigation between passing—falling neatly into the binary of gender—while transgressing it by the very nature of being themselves. Transgender people come out multiple times—in terms of sexuality, gender expression, and identity. It is an evolving process that develops with their self-understanding and a sense of resonance with who they feel they truly are. In this chapter, I discuss how trans men make efforts not just to look like or be perceived as men, but to actually *be* men. In doing this, they navigate fitting in as men while suppressing their transness in order for them to live (van der Wall, 2016). Transgender people have to pass as men or women in order to escape discrimination and also for their own safety. Their decision-making on masculinity, at this stage of their transitioning, is determined by these factors.

Coming Out and Transitioning

Coming out is a fraught process as it involves not only divulging highly personal information about oneself, but doing so in spaces and environments that may be unfriendly and even hostile. In many parts of Asia, coming out is seen as a particularly Western construct built on the experiences of white middle class, urban American citizenship (Huang & Brouwer, 2018, p. 100). Coming out in many places around Asia requires cognisance of the cultural environment one lives in. Exploring the possibility of coming out while maintaining close relations with the heterosexual family home, Chou (2001) suggests that coming home is a process where a person may claim their queer identities while maintaining familial piety and harmony by reining in and concealing queer desires. Thus, being queer and being in a heterosexual marriage and having children are not mutually exclusive to each other; this practice has historical and cultural origins and is accepted in Chinese society.

Where this model may be discomfiting for some, there is the alternate model of coming with, whereby one can live their queer identity without having to conceal it but also without having to declare it out loud (Huang & Brouwer, 2018 p. 108). These alternate models are a necessary consideration to understand that coming out may require different elements of revealing information about oneself, and negotiating the need to conceal some information. This is particularly important in considering the coming out process of transgender people for whom there is constant negotiation between the public and the private. For some, coming out is a private process where only family and close friends are aware of their transgender identity, while the public is not. For others, coming out is a public process where there is a negotiation of the identity when it comes to friends and family. The appeal of the coming home or coming with models is that they are not confrontational and do not offer a dichotomous option of sexuality over family, which critics of the Western coming out model argue does. However, the coming out process for transgender people is confrontational in and of itself as they take on an identity which is almost impossible to conceal due to physical changes. The changes associated with their transitioning pose a challenge to the sex they were assigned at birth and the people who witness these changes are confronted by this, whether the confrontation was intended or not.

LGBTQ people can make various kinds of decisions about how they want to come out. For transgender people, coming out may lead to changes in self-understanding, self-presentation, changes to names and pronouns, or body modifications. Transgender people can make decisions on if and when to make changes and if they make them at all (Vanderburgh, 2014). There are no set ways in which transgender people come out, and the process will differ for each person depending on what each of them decides for themselves. Based on individual needs, the process can be lengthy, affirming, liberating, and positive, albeit messy. This can be seen in LaudeB's telling of his coming out experience:

> I first came out to my sister. Actually I wasn't sure what my "label" was. So I came out to her—I [said I] like girls and all that. But the word lesbian never sat properly with me whenever it was used for me. I was like no I am not a lesbian and then they were like then why are you liking girls and all that. So I came out to my sister [and] then to my aunty. And my aunty did the honour of telling my mother [who is] her sister. I came out to my sister around 2008 telling her that I like girls and all that. And then around 2010–2011 my sister actually told me that she realised that [I] could actually be trans and not a lesbian. And that's when I found there was such a thing as a trans man. And then I did my own research and all that. Then after reading through whatever I read through then that's when I realised I was trans.

LaudeB was out to his family, and he came out to them in stages. He said that coming out, for him, was a process where he made multiple discoveries.

Building his identity on his attraction to women and not knowing about trans men, he believed he was lesbian, although he knew the label did not fit him. Telling his sister about this was pivotal to LaudeB as her exposure to human rights work and language served not only as a source of support but also as a discovery of trans identities. LaudeB said that his mother was also immensely supportive and had since become an ardent and public supporter of transgender rights in Malaysia.

The attraction to women is a significant part of the coming out process for some trans men. Aaron Devor (2004, p. 49) explains that, before realising their trans identity, transgender people come to accept that "the physical sex of their body has mandated their gender status, and they attempt to find ways to successfully navigate between their social expectations and their own needs for self-expression." Thus, transgender people will try to find more comfortable ways to live as their sex assigned at birth while expressing their feelings of belonging to another gender. Assuming they are lesbian is one strategy to reconcile their sexuality before coming to learn that they are men. Another way of accommodating the discrepancy between their assigned sex and their male identity is to take on the tomboy role. John speaks of this when explaining his coming out process:

> When I was small they [suspected I was] a tomboy. They had some questions. I like to be like this. And after I [started] my diploma programme I got to be alone. So that's the time when I [discovered I am] a trans man. I never [told] them anything [at first]. After some months I started to [open up to] my mom and my sister [a] little bit. Because my sister is working as a nurse so she knows about hormones [and] everything. So she's the one who helped my mum to understand this.

John made sense of his family's acceptance of his trans identity by recognising that they had always made space for him being a tomboy. He himself had thought so, too, until he left home and had opportunities to discover his own self along with information on gender identity. Yet, he wanted to come out on his terms and informed his sister first because she was a nurse and she could understand medical transitioning. John's sister became his ally, and she helped him come out to their mother and brother, who had concerns about the hormones that he wanted to be prescribed to begin medical transitioning.

When he spoke to me, John had not yet begun medical transitioning but was socially transitioning and identified as a man. He wanted to become financially stable before embarking on medical transitioning. Transitioning is the term used to refer to the process of changing from one gender presentation to another. Medical transitioning may involve the use of hormones or surgery to make one more comfortable with one's gendered body, while social transitioning may encompass family, work, friends, public persona, legal status, and changes in documentation (Rachlin, 2018, p. 229). It is not uncommon for transgender people to socially transition without undergoing medical transitioning. The transgender rights movement has successfully advocated for people who elect for this mode of transitioning, which has served to challenge the argument that transgender people must experience gender-affirming medical procedures to be considered transgender. This has allowed for an expansion of transgender rights in various parts of the world; trans people may seek to change their gender markers in identity documents without proof of medical procedures marking anatomical changes, for example (Rachlin, 2018).

There is a less common practice of transgender people seeking medical transitioning without social transitioning (Rachlin, 2018). This allows them to publicly present as their sex assigned at birth, but privately enjoy their medically altered bodies. Social transitioning here refers to processes where the person's gender identity is disclosed to others through requests for the use of pronouns or name changes. People may undergo medical procedures that allow them to be more comfortable with their bodies but not require others to acknowledge their gender identities. Transgender people who elect for this mode of transitioning are often seen as "closeted, compromised, or privileged" (Rachlin, 2018, p. 228).

However, their nonconforming bodies—an eschewing of the social expectation that gender is readable and comprehensible—still challenge established gender norms. Transgender people who elect for this mode of transitioning challenge dominant social and medical knowledge of transgender identities, and they pose a challenge to accepted norms and ideas about coming out. John, along with transgender people who medically transition without socially transitioning, show that coming out is not a linear process where one process neatly precedes another in a timely fashion. Coming out is a complex process, and transgender people come out in multiple ways. The coming out process for transgender people is not about gender identity, expression, or sexuality alone but various combinations of each. Recognition of this process has led transgender researchers to make synchronous the process of transitioning with that of self-actualisation, whereby the goal is reaching their true selves (e.g. Goh, 2020).

Stages and Transitions

Before making decisions on transitioning, a transgender person must first recognise and acknowledge that they are transgender. For transgender people, the first coming out process is to themselves. That coming out then leads to self-understanding and developing ways of presenting themselves, as well as pronoun changes and body modifications. Any decision made about this is dependent on that first coming out. That was evident in John's coming out story. I discussed tomboys in previous chapters and how tomboyism is accepted amongst people assigned female at birth as it is indicative of a supposed natural desire for girls to want to experience the greater freedoms and mobilities boys enjoy (Halberstam, 1998, p. 6). This was reflected in John's childhood experience, where his tomboyism was seen as an extension of childhood playfulness and it was allowed. John was also referred to at home by a non-feminine-sounding name,[1] which helped ease the anxieties he felt about his gender identity but could not yet name.

John's experience of being a tomboy as part of his coming out process is also emblematic of Devor's (2004) explanation of transgender people trying on alternative forms of gender expression which would allow them to fit within social expectations of their sex assigned at birth. Proposing a fourteen-stage model of transgender identity formation, Devor (2004) explains that the model is not prescriptive. Neither is there evidence that all transgender people will experience their coming out and transitioning as the model proposes. Some steps may be skipped, and some steps may be revisited and repeated multiple times. The process that one experiences is mediated by personal, familial, social, and environmental factors. Thus, prescribing a process is ill-advised. Factors that determine one's decision are dependent on how congruent they are to that person. Each of these stages is marked by confusion and anxiety, and the aim of decision-making is to reduce the discomfort that comes from those experiences.

For example, based on Devor's model (2004), "identity confusion" (stage 2), akin to that experienced by LaudeB and John, is part of the process of coming out. Sometimes, this confusion can last for a longer period, and the realisation of being transgender can come later. The model proposes that children may come to realise at an early age that there is a disconnect between their identities and their sex assigned at birth, but parents, teachers, and peers will routinely disabuse them of such ideas. This was exemplified

---

1   It is not uncommon in Malaysia for people to have home names which are either a shorter version of their given names, or something different altogether.

in chapters 2 and 3, where trans men provided descriptions of childhood experiences where they were reminded by family and others that they were female and had been socialised as female as well, thus giving rise to cognitive dissonance. The resolution to this situation is transgender people finding "comfortable ways to live as their originally assigned gender while also expressing some of their feelings of belonging to another gender" (Devor, 2004, p. 49).

Gene was another trans man who described identity confusion; as per Devor's model, he experienced identity confusion as a teenager that led him to first think he was a lesbian. He was a 36-year-old Chinese Malaysian. He was partnered with a woman he described as someone he wanted to spend the rest of his life with. He described being socially awkward as a child and being unable to fit in with his peers at school. Gene attended a mixed-sex school and wore the female uniform. He recognised that he had more in common with male students—a love for comics, for example—compared to female students. At the time, he did not realise his trans man identity. He found the community at the church he attended to be more accepting of him and felt less awkward and alone there. However, he was treated as female, and as a teenager, there was an expectation that he would be in a romantic relationship with a boy. He realised at this point that he was not attracted to men, but it was a while before he realised his male identity.

Gene explained that, for a long time, he identified as a lesbian and had a very masculine gender expression. He rationalised that, since he was assigned female at birth and was attracted to women, he must be lesbian. Like LaudeB, at the time Gene first thought he was a lesbian, he did not yet know about trans men. Upon realising his male identity as an adult, he came out to his parents and sister. Gene told me that in October 2015, he sent an email to his family—his parents and his sister—revealing to them his male identity and his decision to begin medical transitioning. His father responded to his email, telling Gene, "It doesn't matter what [he is]." Gene explained that his mother did not directly address his email but began to refer to him with male pronouns and accepted his girlfriend as part of the family. She also slowly stopped commenting on his short hair and his changing body (adding bulk) due to the hormones he was taking for transitioning. He was also out at his workplace where his colleagues refer to and treat him as a man.

Gene's coming out is an example of the non-linear aspect of the coming out process for transgender people; he comes out multiple times. He had first come out as a lesbian to his parents and sister. Gene talked about his parents' journey in accepting his identity. They first accepted him as a lesbian and were open about meeting his girlfriends and treating them as members of their family. Later, Gene came out to them as a trans man, explaining that he was heterosexual as he was attracted to women. Gene said that his father had always treated him like a son—Gene was entrusted with much of the family responsibilities usually assigned to those assigned male at birth in Chinese families. Gene, who does not have a brother, explained that his father positively adapted to Gene's transitioning as male as he could solidify the father-son relationship that he had already begun to foster with Gene.

A significant element in LaudeB's, John's, and Gene's coming out processes is the presence of witnesses. Devor's model suggests that all humans have a need to be witnessed by others for who we are; we want to see ourselves "mirrored in others' eyes as we see ourselves" (2004, p. 46). This process helps us feel validated and confirmed about our sense of self. Witnesses act as powerful reinforcers of transgender identities. LaudeB and John both had their sisters as their witnesses, while Gene had his parents as witnesses to his coming out process. The confidence that they got from being perceived and accepted as men allowed them to come out to others. A crucial factor in determining transgender people's decision-making regarding transitioning, therefore, is to achieve congruence between how others see them and how they see themselves. As such, this process of achieving congruence is an evolving one depending on how people see them—as men or not.

Though presenting a model of transgender identity formation, Devor (2004) argues that the model is not universal nor compulsory for a trans person to follow. This is supported by Dante describing his realisation that he was not lesbian: "I'm not a lesbian. I'm sure. A lesbian is someone that still identify themselves as a female assigned at birth. Well a trans masculine as me identify as boys from inside." Like many of the trans men, Dante's first realisation that he was not like other people assigned female at birth was his attraction to women. Already familiar with the term lesbian, he said that an "inner feeling" made the label of lesbian sit uncomfortably with him. He began to recognise this feeling as being an indicator of his male identity and realised that he was a trans man before calling himself such. He explained that he realised this when he was 15 years old and found that he had more in common with his male friends than female friends, and he could not fit in with girls at school. Dante's decision to identify as a man did not include his decision to come out to his family. He said that his family was conservative and would not understand him, and he was waiting to be financially independent before coming out to his family. He wanted to be ready to be cut off from his family should they insist on him not transitioning.

The other important aspect of Dante's plans on coming out and transitioning was that he valued his sense of congruence between his identity and his physical body. Contrary to the models of coming home (Chou, 2001) and coming with (Huang & Brouwer, 2018), family acceptance or maintaining family harmony is not the primary motivation behind some transgender people's decisions to come out and/or transition. Dorian and Jameel also talked about their willingness to include their families in their transitioning processes and deal with their resistance and transphobia, and arriving at the painful decision to be ready to cut ties with their families if they insisted on them ceasing their transitioning. While they spoke of wanting to have relationships with and be close to their families, they were astute in their view that the family connections will not come at the cost of their own mental health or sense of congruence between their identities and their bodies. Important for trans men like Dante, Dorian, and Jameel is to be accepted for who they are without having limits placed on them by family (or others) regarding the choices they make in becoming the men they want to be.

Transitioning in Safety

The determining factor in trans men's decision to come out and transition with or without family or witnesses is the consideration of their physical safety. Dorian spoke of his experience of wanting to use the male toilet before he began medical transitioning:

> I remember there was this one time I was going to a Deepavali[2] open house and for the first time I put on a jippa.[3] It was a long jippa and I was wearing it to my friend's house. On my way back home I was at the mall and I needed to pee so I was like you know what today I feel grand and I was binding and everything. So I was like I am going to the male toilet. And when I was there a couple of these Indian boys started looking at me and [one of them] [told] his friends oh that's a girl. The queue was so long and I had to wait. I was terrified but I acted as if I didn't understand what the fuck was happening. And I was staring dead ahead. And then a bunch more came and they were staring at me. I backed away slowly and sort of walked away. I thought I don't need this trouble. And I left the toilet and

2   The Festival of Lights celebrated by Hindus.
3   Jippa refers to an Indian-styled tunic usually worn by boys and men.

they started following me. And so I ran. I was like I don't need to know what will happen at the end of this. And they were running after me. Luckily I knew the place well enough to sort of disappear. I don't know what would have happened and I don't want to find out. This experience was enough for me. And at that time my experience with my girlfriend was also enough to remind me that it was not safe. We would go out and people would just stare.

Dorian discussed an experience he had before he transitioned where he was "outed" and experienced the fear of physical violence because of it. Outed, here, refers to an LGBTQ person having information about their sexual orientation or gender identity revealed or discovered without their consent (Schwartz, n.d.). Like other trans men, Dorian described the difficulty of accessing public toilets in Malaysia. Aside from experiencing the discomfort of being watched, he also faced the fear of physical violence from other men (boys) waiting to use the toilet. "I don't know what would have happened and I don't want to find out" is testament to the fear that Dorian felt following this incident at a public male toilet. Going to public toilets poses a problem for transgender people as they are policed by both men and women. The trans men had shared their experiences of being policed when accessing the women's toilet and the fear of being policed when accessing the men's toilet. They described having had security guards knock on the door of the cubicle that they were in to check if they are male or female, or older women (especially janitors) stopping them when they entered the women's toilet pre-transitioning. It was usually their voice that gave away the fact that they were assigned female at birth. Upon hearing their voices, the security guards were apologetic, and the women in the public toilet became visibly less anxious.

Trans men typically lose the ability to allay threats in female public toilets when they begin medical transitioning and their voices change and take on more masculine tones. They then face the fear of violence should they be discovered when they are in the men's toilet. Highly contested spaces, bathrooms are a form of technology of disciplinary power (Bender-Baird, 2016, p. 984) designed to inadvertently police gender. The sex-segregated bathroom introduces a design that facilitates and encourages surveillance, thus producing docile and appropriately gendered bodies. Violation of the rules that operate for using the toilets disrupts the presumed naturalness of the man-masculinity/woman-femininity binary, thus allowing for abusive comments, exclusions, and physical violence (Browne, 2004, p. 332).

REALISING MALE IDENTITY   81

Trans men who described experiences of being policed in women's bathrooms bring to mind Halberstam's (1998, p. 20) discussion of the bathroom problem. The bathroom problem posits that having one's gender challenged in women's toilets is a frequent occurrence for androgynous or masculine women. In public toilets for women, various users tend to fail to measure up to expectations of femininity, and people who present in some ambiguous way are routinely questioned and challenged about their presence in the "wrong" bathroom (Halberstam, 1998, p. 23). Androgynous and masculine women fail at being readable at a glance; the successful performance of gender involves the observer being able to read and accept the other person's gender. Failure for this to happen results in violence—verbal or physical, real or the threat of. Trans men's use of men's bathrooms rests on their ability to pass. Trans men such as Liw and Kyle attest to this when they speak of not ever having experienced policing when they use the men's toilets despite being wary of it. This could also be due to men not being as vigilant about intruders in the toilet as women are (1998, p. 25), and Liw and Kyle not experiencing scrutiny of their gender expression in men's toilets.

Successful passing, for trans men, means that they have achieved the kind of masculinity that signals a flight from women and the repudiation of femininity (Kimmel, 2006). A psychological unpacking of male role norms (Thompson & Pleck, 1986, p. 534) offers three aspects: men's need to achieve status and others' respect (status norms); expectations that men should be mentally, emotionally, and physically tough and self-reliant ("toughness" norms); and expectations that men should avoid stereotypically feminine activities and occupations ("anti-femininity" norms). The boys that Dorian encountered perceived him as female and needed to expel him from the masculine space (waiting in line in the men's toilet) in order to declare and assert their own masculinity and maleness. Dorian's presence there did not just disrupt the perceived gender binary, but also the boys' own sense of being male and masculine. It was also a demonstration of the other boys displaying their masculinity in a way to ascertain (or demonstrate) their position in the hierarchy of masculinities.

Discussions of gender and bathrooms must also take into consideration the protection of such spaces for the purported safety of cisgender women and children. Fears related to transgender people in women's bathrooms have been referred to as penis panic (Schilt & Westbrook, 2015, p. 27). The fears have resulted in gender policing in women's bathrooms, which are antithetical to the idea of equality as it assumes that women and children are victims in need of protection and that men are inherent rapists (Schilt & Westbrook, 2015, p. 27). Trans men, on the other hand, are viewed as women because they do not possess a "natural penis" (Schilt & Westbrook, 2015, p. 30) and, therefore, are not viewed as potential threats to women and yet are not regarded as women. A fully transitioned trans man is still not considered a man as his penis is not "natural." It thus becomes necessary for trans men to pass as men in order to safely use public toilets, and, in this sense, it will have to be the men's toilet.

This circuitous argument harks back to transgender people wanting to pass in order to be read as not trans. They want to be seen as male/men or female/women and blend in to become unnoticeable, thus being read as real men or women amongst the general public (van der Wall, 2016). As can be seen from Dorian's experience, not being perceived as a "real" man has dire consequences for transgender people. Passing is directly linked to the degree of precariousness a trans person may be exposed to. Precarity is directly linked with gender norms, and those who do not live their genders in intelligible ways are at heightened risk of harassment and violence (Butler, 2009, p. ii). Hence, trans men's decision-making about coming out and transitioning is also based on how well they pass and how much safety that offers them. Coming out for transgender people is multidimensional, and is not just about coming out with regard to one's sexuality, but coming out about one's self. This process, as exemplified by trans men's testimonies in this study, happens again and again, over time and in different ways (Bong, 2020, p. 119).

The coming out process is non-linear. Goh (2020, p. 5) articulates this wonderfully by capturing that the essence of becoming trans men is to "*become* [italics are author's own], and never to be as fait accompli even if *being* [italics are author's own] is an aspiration of 'successful' ontological achievement." It is an evolving process where the starting point often changes but sometimes is the same. Furthermore, it is as much dependent on what and how the trans man feels—how much he is passing, or not, and how much congruence with gender expression he is experiencing—as it does on factors such as access to and availability of medical and social transitioning. In agreeing with Goh (2020), I resist the temptation to describe the coming out process in stages in order to fully account for the complexities of the processes of becoming. Also to consider in the transitioning process for trans men in Malaysia is the lack of legal gender recognition. Transgender people in Malaysia cannot change the gender markers in their legal documents, which poses a challenge to their transitioning processes. Regardless of their identities as men, the law still regards them as women. Access to gender-affirming medical procedures in Malaysia remains an issue impacting the human rights of transgender people. For many transgender people, gender-affirming medical procedures

REALISING MALE IDENTITY   83

can only be accessed through the private medical system or abroad, making it expensive and inaccessible to many.

Trans men in Malaysia may not be able to be overtly out at all times as a means of protection or self-preservation. Choosing silence is not a complicit strategy to remain in the closet. It is, instead, a necessary part of transgender people's processes of coming out that involves deciphering safety and negotiating social situations. Passing requires silence, which is necessary for the safety and dignity of transgender people. Other decisions also need to be made in order for trans men to successfully pass in Malaysia, which will be explored in the following section.

Passing as Men

Successful passing for a trans man is to become an invisible man by becoming a visible man (Bong, 2020). He must undergo physical changes—top surgery (removal of breasts), voice change, changes in musculature—in order to be perceived as a man. Passing is seen as an achievement for transgender people—they have been able to be accepted as "just" men or women. For trans men, it means being able to use the men's bathroom without fear of being discovered.

To do this, trans men need to embody masculinity in their journeys of becoming men. They go through this phase as a means of acculturating themselves to being men after living and being socialised as women. To do this, they may enact the more typically stereotyped ideas of men and masculinity in their efforts to pass and be seen as men. An example of this can be seen in Miles's experience where, after coming out and starting his transition, he became very self-conscious about his behaviour:

> I think for the first few months I was even more aware of [whether] I wasn't performing masculinity [If I had a moment of] I won't say feminine but like just on the spectrum, it's not as masculine then I would be very self-conscious and I would be like oh no I don't want people to misread who I am. So I would dial it back down or like I would shut it down quickly. But I was very aware.

Miles described a self-policing of his behaviours for fear that he would not be perceived by others as a man. This means that he had to "dial down" his femininity and perform a certain kind of masculinity in order to pass and be accepted as a man. Miles demonstrates the performative element of gender, where it is always a doing (Butler, 1999). The performance must also be coherent and make sense to others. The need to perform is felt even more when he is in the company of other men. He says:

> Sometimes if I'm hanging out with a bunch of cis men there comes a need to seem a certain way in order to be part of the conversation and I find myself performing that because that's not normally how I behave outside of these circles. Even [when I am] with trans men also actually.

Miles's description of how he behaves around other men (cis and trans men) is emblematic of how homosocial environments affirm and control gender identity and expression—in this case, masculinity. Homosociality is the social bonds between people of the same sex (Bird, 1996). While homosocial bonds apply to men and women, it is men's lives that are said to be highly organised by relations between them, where males seek the approval of other males (Flood, 2008). By altering his behaviour "to be part of the conversation," Miles made decisions to behave in certain ways to be accepted by the men he was with. Acceptance, for him, signified approval of his masculinity and that he is seen as a man. To do this, Miles also became vigilant about how he moves his body. He said:

> I noticed that I stopped dancing in the first one and a half years on testosterone. I just refused to dance because before I had testosterone in me I would just dance. I didn't care. Whatever my body wants to move, it will just move but when I was on testosterone I realised like wow I cannot like what if people can still see that female side of me or whatever. So I just refused to dance.

To avoid being seen as a trans man, Miles had to police himself and become hypervigilant about how he moves his body. For men, the body signifies manhood and how it is being used becomes proof of that manhood. It is marked by social discourse and different life events, all acting in tandem to signal manhood (Mellstrom, 2002). For trans men like Miles, beginning to identify as men and medically transitioning (Miles was on testosterone hormone therapy) are life events that signal the changing social discourse of his body. Miles is no longer female, and, as a male person, he must perform as such.

Masculinity is defined, in a binary fashion, by its distance from femininity. Anti-femininity is one of three constituting male norms of masculinity (Thompson & Pleck, 1986). Both of Miles's quotes highlight his need to distance himself from femininity for him to be seen as male. Most evident of these, for Miles, is how he moves his body. Evidence indicates that the correlation between masculinity, status, and toughness has changed, but the anti-femininity sentiment remains (Fischer et al., 1998). As the concept of masculinity is inherently relational, it cannot exist except in contrast with femininity. Hence, Miles can only show that he is masculine by not being feminine. His performance of masculinity lies in his distancing from and not performing femininity.

Butler (1999) has argued that the performance of gender has two elements. The first is "the way in which the anticipation of a gendered essence produces that which it posits as outside itself"; and the second is that it is not a single act but "a repetition and a ritual, which achieves its effects through its naturalisation in the context of a body, understood in part, as a culturally sustained temporal duration" (Butler, 1999, p. xv). By this definition, trans men's experience of an "inner feeling" of being men (as cited by Dante above) provides them with a sense of how men are expected to behave, thus leading them to enact repetitions of certain behaviours that are socially sanctioned as masculine. This assumes that trans men have a pre-existing set of ideas or information sets of men's behaviours. One possible way to describe this pre-existing set of ideas of men's behaviours is heuristics.

Two common examples of heuristics are availability heuristics and representativeness heuristics. For availability heuristics, individual instances of information are retrieved, and a judgement of the amount or frequency of certain information determines the ease and frequency of its retrieval (Hastie & Dawes, 2001, p. 117). Representativeness heuristics, on the other hand, require the retrieval of information about generic concepts and a similarity match assessment is made, comparing the original to-be-judged case with the category (Hastie & Dawes, 2001, p. 117). This process relies on how well a case matches with existing information stored in a person's memory.

When people use heuristics, the ones they use will depend on the cues they perceive in the situation and on the habit strength of activating that heuristic compared to other heuristics (O'Neil et al., 2017). The more frequently an individual uses a heuristic, the likelier it is to be activated. In Miles's example, activation of the ways in which he performed masculinity was dependent on how much others thought he was a man ("I don't want people to misread me"), and how those heuristics were reinforced by others—the validation of those heuristics by others, especially men.

There are many ways in which these heuristics are formed. Shane spoke of his experiences of learning what men are supposed to do and not do. He was a 32-year-old Chinese Malaysian teacher. He told me of an incident where he held the door open for his male friends because it was what he was used to doing:

> Some of them do come up to me and be like dude why [are] you so nice. Then I'm like what you mean. They're like oh nobody open[ed] door for me before [and] like dude I can open [the] door by myself. And I was like yeah but I'm opening [the] door for everybody already. He's like yeah but I can open it. I was like okay. So, the next time we go out if I open the door, sometimes I have to consciously say let go of the door [and] let it close and then let them open it themselves.

Based on the idea of masculinity as a heuristic, Shane opens the door for his male friends because that has become a habit. It is an act that has high habit strength. However, he has to learn to activate a new set of heuristics pertaining to "men don't open doors for other men" in order to fit in with his male friends, even if the behaviour is a cultural norm and not a gendered one. Shane has had to learn to change his ideas of being a man based on the feedback he receives from others. The negative response that his behaviours elicit influences the decisions he makes on how he embodies his masculine identity. Drawing from Michael Flood's (2008) argument that males seek the approval of other males, the reprimands or feedback that Shane receives from his male friends play a big role in how he makes decisions on the kind of masculinity he embodies. Aside from learning about masculinity, these behaviours also mark Shane's hierarchical position amongst men. Such markers of manhood improve men's position in social hierarchies (Kimmel, 2006). Shane is positioned higher or lower amongst men based on how masculine they deem his behaviour. Seeking approval from other men also means that Shane is now involved in this hierarchising process.

Learning to Be Men

The development of these heuristics is explained by social learning theory (Bandura, 1973), which provides the understanding that human behaviours are learnt and are not innate. Modelling other people's behaviour is a crucial element in learning; responses are learnt through example. Social learning theory demonstrates that same-sex modelling is present in very young children where they can distinguish activities that are stereotypical for each sex and can judge same-sex models that are appropriate for them to adopt (Bussey & Bandura, 1984). Children learn and engage in the processes of encoding, organising, and retrieving information about themselves and others to develop gender schemas. However, same-sex modelling is not simply about children repeating the behavioural patterns of male and female role models. There is a selective element in the process of retrieval and enactment of behaviours, where these are chosen from both sexes.

Hence, heuristics of masculinity (and femininity), as well as appropriate gender performance, are learnt not by separating men's and women's behaviours but by coding everybody's behaviours and only then coding these by gender. These become representative heuristics and their use by trans men in decision-making about masculinity can be exemplified by Mitch's description of observing his parents when he was growing up:

> My mom nags. She's so loud. My mom was the queen who [held] the house together. But I just couldn't take what she was doing at that point in time. All [that] nagging and all [that] noise. And yes she does what a mother would do but there was something about my dad. That calm quiet way [where] my mom nags and he [would] turn to all of us and say yeah it's okay your mom wants the best for you. You know. And he was that calming factor in the family.

His mother was a housewife while his father was a police officer. Mitch said that the men in his family have a quiet way of showing their affections. His father was the calming factor in his home. His grandfather showed his affection by making sure that when his grandchildren visited him in the *kampung*[4] he would have their favourite breakfast food, *nasi lemak*,[5] bought and ready before they woke up. He described having grown up admiring these aspects of their personalities. He was clear that he wanted to be like his father and grandfather and not like his mother. He wanted to emulate those qualities with his children.

Mitch's description exemplified how children learn gender by gleaning information from men and women. However, same-sex modelling is more common amongst boys, while girls are influenced by male and female models (Bussey & Bandura, 1984, p. 1300). The determining factor on whose behaviour is modelled is dependent on how much power that person is

---

4   A Malay Malaysian village.
5   A Malaysian dish where the rice is cooked in coconut milk and served with spicy relish and condiments.

perceived to have. Applying this to Mitch's perception of his parents' behaviours suggests that he not only found his mother's behaviours unlikable but also perceived his father as having more power in the relationship, despite his mother being the "queen" of the house. Power, in this sense, is not determined by authority but by the ability and resources to reward others (Bussey & Bandura, 1984). Also important is feedback on behaviours and their subsequent reinforcement. Mitch's experience of his mother's behaviours was negative; hence, he is less likely to repeat them. Since he experienced his father's behaviours positively, he is more likely to repeat these.

The reinforcement of certain behaviours can also be social factors such as attaining romantic interest. Miles told me how he would pay attention when his female friends spoke of their experiences with men. He said: "Because I was thinking [that since] I'm not biologically male I [would] have to compensate by being better [than cis men]. So whatever [female friends] didn't like in their male partners I would be the exact opposite of that." Before coming out as a trans man, Miles thought he was a lesbian. Like the others, he thought this as he had not yet learnt about trans men. Also, he had to be clandestine about his identity when he was growing up because the religious community he belonged to believed that being LGBTQ was wrong. He explained that being a lesbian was a safe way he could express his identity and sexuality as there was less scrutiny of relationships between women in his church. Impressing women was then a big motivation for him. This was an early influence on his decision-making with regard to how he embodied masculinity. He explained that this helped him become more confident as a man. The things he learnt from his female friends' descriptions formed some of the heuristics that Miles developed about men.

Much of the work on understanding children's behaviours about and around gender are based on the idea that there are two genders and assumes that children assigned fe/male at birth will model others assigned fe/male at birth. Based on current understanding of sex and gender, and the position on gender and sexuality I take in this study, the flaws in this understanding should be apparent. Yet, such findings can still be valued for the principles of social learning theory that they propose. The argument that I forwarded in chapter 2 lays the ground for the assumption that trans men identified as male early in life and therefore looked to their fathers and other male members of their family to learn about and understand masculinity, as Mitch (and Cunie, as seen in chapter 3) do. In being socialised as female (chapter 3), the trans men also learnt that being male is the binaric opposite of being female.

There is also value in the social learning theory of gender as it cautions against viewing social learning as purely mimicking. Hans and Liw's experiences are emblematic of that. Hans told me about his decision to learn about being a man by watching other men:

> There was one time I decided to sit somewhere and watch men. You know how they talk to people, their body language. And actually also a friend told me that maybe I should open up. I mean my body language. And they said that men tend to spread. So they said that maybe if you do this more you won't feel so small between them.

Similarly, Liw told me how he learnt certain rules with regard to being a man in Malaysia. He was a 31-year-old self-employed Chinese Malaysian. He said he managed to pass by observing and mimicking men's behaviours:

> Malay guys only shake hands [with other] guys, not women. So, to pass better I need to remember to give [men] the handshake because they always shake their hand. And pat on the shoulder things like that. This is what I learn along the way.

For both Hans and Liw, a big element of learning to behave like men is to feel more comfortable with themselves, and to manage their fears of being discovered as trans. To learn the nuances of men's behaviours, Liw tacitly observed them while Hans decided to actively watch them. Modelling behaviour is heavily impacted by the anticipated consequences of behaviours (Anderson & Kras, 2005, p. 104). Hence, Liw was comfortable perpetuating some of the behaviours he saw as it served his purpose of passing and was rewarding. Blending in meant that he faced less scrutiny in public, which made him less self-aware and more confident. The impact for Liw is that when he and his girlfriend were out in public together they were less likely to be stared at and feel unsafe. He said:

> When I go out there's not so many eyes looking at me, especially when I am with my girlfriend. When we [used to] go out last time as a lesbian couple we will get a lot of attention. After transitioning I feel much at peace.

However, Liw exercised discernment in the behaviours he chose to model. He had to identify the nuances of masculine behaviours based on accepted norms in the different racial groups and religious mores in Malaysia. In that same vein, Gene also exercised his judgement on the kinds of masculine behaviours he wanted to model. Unlike Mitch, Gene did not want to be the kind of man his father was. He said:

> I love my dad. I just don't want to worship my dad. I have found different role models who are more aligned with me. I just believe my dad is a product of his time. He does embody a lot of toxic masculinity.

Gene described his father as being the eldest son in his traditional Chinese family. His father was appointed as head of the family after his own father's death. Gene described how his grandmother would have his father sit at the head of the table and be served first and be given the choice pieces of meat that was cooked. Gene disagreed with such treatment of men in families. He used the term "toxic masculinity," which has come to be used to describe the most extreme versions of hyper masculine communities of practice characterised by homophobia and the domination and subjugation of weaker men and women (Creighton & Oliffe, 2010, p. 414). Toxic masculinity has been linked to aggressive and predatory heterosexual behaviour resulting in sexual and domestic violence perpetrated by men (Bhana, 2012), the suppression of men's emotions leading to mental health issues (Addis & Cohane, 2005), and men's engagement in masculinism and men's rights activism (Banet-Weiser & Miltner, 2016). Toxic masculinity is about exhibiting power and control over others who are deemed less powerful. Gene decided that he did not want to emulate this kind of masculinity. He chose against modelling behaviours aligned with male power. Instead, he made decisions that favour prosocial behaviours and attitudes, where he could also feel good about himself.

The advantage of trans men treating masculinity as a set of heuristics is that it helps them feel like they fit in. While beneficial as a means of quick decision-making and problem-solving, over-reliance on heuristics can lead to poor outcomes when people jump to conclusions based on limited evidence that they have immediately available (Kahneman, 2011). A heuristic can become overused, leading to developing the "is-ought fallacy," i.e. "because this is how men must behave, and the evidence for the same is all around me, then I also ought to behave this way" (O'Neil et al., 2017, p. 86). This is how behaviours, especially gendered behaviours, become stereotypes.

Daniel Kahneman's (2011) systems theory of cognition also influences decision-making processes involved in performing masculinity. System 1 thinking is automatic and unconscious, emotional, and intuitive. It reacts quickly to the environment and quickly produces responses in reaction to incoming stimuli. System 1 thinking guides responses to the environment as quickly as possible. Through automatic application, a relevant heuristic guides behaviour based on simple and unexamined decision rules. This serves an evolutionary purpose as it increases the likelihood of survival in various situations. Applied to transgender people, it becomes understandable that they would adopt this mode of decision-making as it not only helps them pass but also keeps them safe from physical violence. The feelings and emotions crucial in making transgender people feel safe are an essential element in decision-making. Emotions activate mindsets whereby they activate cognitive procedures or sets of mental associations that they then automatically apply to tasks conducted under the emotion's influence. System 2 thinking, on the other hand, is effortful, slow, and more reflective, and requires a different set of processes for decision-making that I will elaborate in chapter 7.

Passing is a crucial factor influencing trans men's decision-making regarding masculinity. Denying or repudiating the feminine is an expectation of masculinity which plays a role in confirming trans men's identities as men at this stage of their transitioning. Trans men want to be perceived as men and not as trans men as much for their own feelings of safety as well as for the development of their identities. They transform their bodies to resemble cisgender men and perform masculinity in ways that establishes themselves as men, leaving them with having to decide what to do with their female histories. Since masculinity is defined by its distance from femininity, its focus is more on what it is not rather than what it is. Trans men passing as men demonstrate that they do not mimic men but utilise active cognitive processes that require an understanding of power, relations, and factors in their environment. The following chapter will explore how these decision-making processes are tested and then change in their relationships with men and women.

References

Addis, M., & Cohane, G. (2005). Social scientific paradigms of masculinity and their implications for research and practice in men's mental health. *Journal of Clinical Psychology, 61*(6), 633–647. https://doi.org/10.1002/jclp.20099

Anderson, J. F., & Kras, K. (2005). Revisiting Albert Bandura's social learning theory to better understand and assist victims of intimate personal violence. *Women & Criminal Justice, 17*(1), 99–124. https://doi.org/10.1300/J012v17n01_05

Bandura, A. (1973). *Aggression: A social learning analysis*. Prentice Hall.

Banet-Weiser, S., & Miltner, K. M. (2016). #MasculinitySoFragile: Culture, structure and networked misogyny. *Feminist Media Studies, 16*(1), 171–174. https://doi.org/10.1080/14680777.2016.1120490

Bender-Baird, K. (2016). Peeing under surveillance: Bathroom, gender policing and hate violence. *Gender, Place & Culture, 23*(7), 983–988. https://doi.org/10.1080/0966369X.2015.1073699

Bhana, D. (2012). Girls are not free: In and out of the South African school. *International Journal of Educational Development, 32*(2), 352–358. https://doi.org/10.1016/j.ijedudev.2011.06.002

Bird, S. R. (1996). Welcome to the men's club: Homosociality and the maintenance of hegemonic masculinity. *Gender & Society, 10*(2), 120–132. https://doi.org/10.1177/089124396010002002

Bong, S. A. (2020). *Becoming queer and religious in Malaysia and Singapore.* Bloomsbury.

Browne, K. (2004). Genderism and the bathroom problem: (Re)materialising sexed sites, (re)creating sexed bodies. *Gender, Place & Culture, 11*(3), 331–346. https://doi.org/10.1080/0966369042000258668

Bussey, K., & Bandura, A. (1984). Influence of gender constancy and social power on sex-linked modelling. *Journal of Personality and Social Psychology, 47*(6), 1292–1302. https://doi.org/10.1037/0022-3514.47.6.1292

Butler, J. (1999). *Gender trouble.* Routledge.

Butler, J. (2009). Performativity, precarity and sexual politics. *AIBR Revista De Antropologia Iberoamericana, 4*(3), 321–336. http://www.aibr.org/antropologia/netesp/

Chou, W-S. (2001). Homosexuality and the cultural politics of *tongzhi* in Chinese society. *Journal of Homosexuality, 40*(3–4), 27–46. https://doi.org/10.1300/J082v40n03_03

Creighton, G., & Oliffe, J. L. (2010). Theorising men's health: A brief history with a view to practice. *Health Sociology Review, 19*(4), 409–418. https://doi.org/10.5172/hesr.2010.19.4.409

Devor, A. H. (2004). Witnessing and mirroring: A fourteen stage model of transsexual identity formation. *Journal of Gay and Lesbian Psychotherapy, 8*(1–2), 41–67. https://www.tandfonline.com/doi/abs/10.1300/J236v08n01_05

Fischer, A. R., Tokar, D. M., Good, G. E., & Snell, A. F. (1998). More on the role of male norms: Exploratory and multiple sample confirmatory analyses. *Psychology of Women Quarterly, 22*(2), 135–155. https://doi.org/10.1111/j.1471-6402.1998.tb00147.x

Flood, M. (2008). Men, sex and homosociality: How bonds between men shape their sexual relations with women. *Men and Masculinities, 10*(3), 339–359. https://doi.org/10.1177/1097184X06287761

Goh, J. N. (2020). *Becoming a Malaysian trans man: Gender, society, body and faith.* Palgrave Macmillan.

Halberstam, J. (1998). *Female masculinity*. Duke University Press.

Hastie, R., & Dawes, R. M. (2001). *Rational choice in an uncertain world: The psychology of judgment and decision making*. Sage Publications.

Huang, S., & Brouwer, D. C. (2018). Coming out, coming home, coming with: Model of queer sexuality in contemporary China. *Journal of International and Intercultural Communication, 11*(2), 97–116. https://doi.org/10.1080/17513057.2017.1414867

Kahneman, D. (2011). *Thinking, fast and slow*. Penguin.

Kimmel, M. (2006). *Manhood in America: A cultural history*. The Free Press.

Mellstrom, U. (2002). Patriarchal machines and masculine embodiment. *Science, Technology and Human Values, 27*(4), 460–478. https://doi.org/10.1177/016224302236177

O'Neil, J., Wester, S. R., Heesacker, M., & Snowden, S. J. (2017). Masculinity as a heuristic: Gender role conflict theory, superorganisms, and system-level thinking. In R. F. Levant & Y. J. Wong (Eds.), *The psychology of men and masculinities* (pp. 75–103). American Psychological Association. https://doi.org/10.1037/0000023-004

Rachlin, K. (2018). Medical transition without social transition. *TSQ: Transgender Studies Quarterly, 5*(2), 228–244. https://doi.org/10.1215/23289252-4348660

Schilt, K., & Westbrook, L. (2015). Bathroom battlegrounds and penis attacks. *Contexts, 14*(3), 26–31. https://doi.org/10.1177/1536504215596943

Schwartz, A. P. (n.d.). *Why outing can be deadly*. National LGBTQ Taskforce. https://www.thetaskforce.org/why-outing-can-be-deadly/

Thompson, E. H., & Pleck, J. H. (1986). The structure of male role norms. *The American Behavioural Scientist, 29*(5), 531–543. https://doi.org/10.1177/000276486029005003

van der Wall, E. (2016) Crossing over, coming out, blending in: A trans interrogation of the closet. *South African Review of Sociology, 47*(3), 44–64. https://doi.org/10.1080/21528586.2016.1163289

Vanderburgh, R. (2014). Coming out. In L. Erickson-Schroth (Ed.), *Trans bodies, trans selves: A resource for the transgender community* (pp. 105–123). Oxford University Press.

5.   Experiencing Masculinity

Abstract: In enquiring how trans men make decisions about the kind(s) of masculinity they want to express, this chapter continues to address the second of three aspects, where they proclaim their male identities and perform masculinity in order to be accepted by other men and women. This chapter first examines the role played by gender stereotypes in homosocial and heterosocial relationships. It also begins to examine interviewees' relationships with their female histories as they come to recognise that these play a role in their decision-making about masculinity.

Keywords: trans men, Malaysia, decision-making, female histories, homosocial

Passing and cognitive tools such as masculinity as heuristics enable trans men to move and be in the world as men. They are less likely to be "clocked" and read as female and can engage with others as men, leading them to different experiences of relationships with women and other men. The impact of these relations with men and women brings them to relate to their own masculinities and identities differently. This requires a new phase of decision-making as they discover that gender is not a state of them being men but is relational and dependent on how they interact with others (e.g. Connell, 1995). Masculinity is experienced as being manifested in the various processes and relationships through which men and women conduct their gendered lives. Trans men come to see that masculinity only exists in relation to femininity enacted through symbolic differences, pitting the two genders in a state of binaric complementarity.

Through experiencing this relational nature of gender, trans men receive information that they can, in turn, use to either enforce existing notions of gender meanings or weaken them. Here, also, there is an active process of deciphering information instead of a passive receiving to replicate it akin to play-acting. I propose that trans men use interactions with cisgender

---

Kumaresan, Vizla. *Trans Men in Malaysia: Decision-Making, Masculinity and Manhood.* Amsterdam: Amsterdam University Press, 2025.
DOI: 10.5117/9789048562596_CH05

men to learn the ways of being men. These homosocial interactions are a necessary step for them to develop experiences that will either affirm their ideas of manhood or challenge them.

Experiencing Relationships with Men

Flood (2008, p. 342) identifies four ways that homosociality organises "the male-female sociosexual relations" of heterosexual men: (1) male-male relationships take priority over male-female relations, and platonic friendships with women are feminising and therefore dangerous and rare; (2) sexual activity is a key path to masculine status where other men are the audience, imagined or real; (3) heterosexual sex can be the medium through which male bonding is enacted; and (4) men's sexual storytelling is shaped by homosocial masculine cultures. Relationships between men, therefore, serve the purpose of reinforcing the idea that that which is feminine is removed from that which is masculine. The feminine has to be objectified and othered, and sometimes it is necessary to humiliate and dehumanise women in order to achieve this (Flood, 2008).

However, homosocial relations can also be affirming for men as they provide affirmation that they are doing gender properly (Schrock & Schwalbe, 2009, p. 281). This is evident in Blue's experience, where he described a change in his relationships with men post-transition. Blue told me that he found it easier to fit in with the men he worked with after starting his transitioning process:

> [At] work I deal with contractors. Again, contractors are mostly men, like uncles.[1] And before transition, they would [perceive] me like they think that I am inexperienced or they would see me like maybe I'm unsure of things but now I would say this or that and they would be like, "Oh, okay." And they have no questions of why I'm doing these things. Before they would ask like "Oh, are you sure you wanna do this?" They stopped doubting me.

Blue found it remarkable that the men he worked with in the interior design industry—colleagues and contractors—no longer second-guessed his decisions and extended respect to him. They never asked Blue about the physical changes that came with his transitioning—the change in his voice, especially. They very quickly adopted the use of male pronouns

---

1   A common term in Malaysia to refer to older men.

with him. Blue also said that his cis male friends treated him differently. Where they kept him at a distance before ("They talk to me about work"), Blue began to sense more intimacy. He said, "They would talk to me like a friend. And there is physical touch now because they think it is okay to touch me." They did not touch him previously because he was perceived as female. That they touched him after transitioning indicated to Blue that these cis men accepted him as a man.

Blue's description of the friendship he had developed with his cis male friends is emblematic of "bromance," which is marked by emotionally intense bonds between straight men (DeAngelis, 2014, p. 1). Moving away from a model of male stoicism, the emotional nuance of the bromance is perceived as an indication of the changing nature of relationships between men. Aside from Blue, Dines experienced this in his friendships with cis men, too. His older friends knew of his transitioning process, and Dines told me they did not voice any dissent to it. Instead, they learnt his preferred pronouns and referred to him as "bro." Dines had also come to be surprised by the sensitivity displayed by some of these cisgender men. For instance, they could sense when he was uncomfortable when someone asked him about his voice. They would then change the subject or step up for him.

Observers have attributed intimacy in bromances to the shift in the masculine socialisation process along with the advocacy around homosexuality that has reduced men's stigma of being perceived as gay (Robinson et al, 2017, p. 95). The fear of socially being perceived as gay—homohysteria—meant that men's friendships used to focus on being engaged with each other while doing activities with little room for self-disclosure, which is an integral aspect of fostering emotional intimacy. Studies of American undergraduate male friendships indicate that younger men are more open to discussing feelings with friends without the fear of being perceived as gay. Shared interests are still a cornerstone of these friendships, but it is physical and emotional intimacy that is crucial for enjoyment in these relationships.

Intimacy with men is also something that Jervind recognised he could have after starting his transitioning. Jervind began medically transitioning with testosterone hormones and had his top surgery, i.e. double mastectomy. His friends regarded him as male and used his preferred pronouns. He told me about his experience going for a massage at a parlour he did not realise provided "extra service":

> So [she] thought that I am [a cis] man. [She] wanted to pull down my pants. And wanted [to give me a] hand job, I think. [She] even [asked me if I wanted a] hand job or blow job. They will provide this service. I

> [said no]. Then I asked my [guy] friends. Usually [when] you guys go [to massage parlours] [do] they offer [this to] you or not? They said of course. If you go alone [or] if [there is no woman] beside [you] of course. Usually single men will go there [for sexual pleasure].

Jervind informed me that his cisgender male friends responded with a nonchalant "Oh? Ok," when he told them that he was a trans man. He and his friends regularly travelled together, and his experience in the quote above was at a massage parlour during one of those trips abroad. Though relieved that the masseuse perceived him as a man, Jervind was quite shaken by the experience. He said he could only discuss it with his male friends. His attempts to share this experience with his female friends elicited responses of disgust ("Ee yer"[2]), and he recognised that "it's not a right topic to talk" about with them.

From his male friends, Jervind learnt some aspects of living as a man. For instance, he learnt to be discerning about the massage parlours he patronised. He also learnt to debunk his beliefs about sex. One of these was his long-held notion that sexual activities happen only at night; "I said it [was] afternoon [and] not at night. They [said] anytime. No need to see time." Peer relationships between men are supposed to provide information about how men are to conduct their relationships—platonic or not—with women. Although Jervind had a girlfriend whom he had been with since before he transitioned, he now has to learn to navigate relations with women as a man.

Jervind recognised that his relationships with his female friends would now be different. He was cautious about what he spoke about when he was with them, while he did not find the need to censor himself when he was with his male friends. He felt that his conversations with his male friends were "more open. Whatever we want to mention [we] just say it." Patterns of communication in young men's relationships with each other reveal that they work within the parameters of appropriate forms of masculinity within their close friendships, which draw on various discursive strategies, including insults, silences, and direct integration when connecting with each other (McDiarmid et al., 2016, p. 358).

Ideas of masculinity such as "hardness, toughness, coolness, competitiveness, dominance and control" make it hard to signal friendship and solidarity (McDiarmid et al., 2016, p. 358). This does not mean men cannot attain that in their friendships. They develop their own means of expressing connection with other men, which have been found to be sophisticated verbal and nonverbal communication styles and patterns (McDiarmid et

---

2   A common response in Malaysian parlance indicating disgust.

al., 2016, p. 358). However, because these communication patterns serve to maintain the ideals of masculinity, particularly that of anti-femininity, these communication patterns can be sexist and misogynistic. When pressed, Jervind could not articulate exactly what topics he and his male friends self-censor when they are with their female friends. However, by not examining the women's discomfort, Jervind and his male friends inadvertently maintained and perpetuated the boundaries that separate men and women, thus establishing the anti-feminine qualities of masculinity.

Jervind's sharing of the incident at the massage parlour was treated lightly by his male friends. The sharing could have been assumed to be a way of bonding between them. It may also have been seen as a symbol of success that Jervind was perceived as male. That also lends him status amongst his male peers. Men's status is not measured solely by whether they achieve intercourse but is organised in terms of wider hierarchies of sexual practices and the social coding of sexed bodies (Flood, 2008, p. 346). Men are assigned status based on how much and what kinds of heterosexual sexual experiences they have. Bragging amongst men about one's sexual activities with women is a way of attaining status and an indication of achievement of masculinity.

Sex and Masculinity

Jervind's friends seem to have normalised the fact that it is not uncommon for men to experience these kinds of sexual acts at massage parlours. Jervind told me, "But [the female masseuses are] really sexy. I think if I am a man I will go for it." For Jervind, the only thing that held him back that day was that he had not had a phalloplasty and, therefore, was not a man. However, it did not strike him that the masseuse perceived him as a man; he had demonstrated and adequately performed masculinity and manhood for her, and she had responded in the way she would with any other male client. Men are typically defined as "biological males" who are complete if they have the attending biological requirements: XY chromosomes, male reproductive organs, and a [sexually viable] penis (Schrock & Schwalbe, 2009, p. 279). Hence, Jervind's understanding of a "real man" was concordant with this idea. As I discussed in chapter 4, trans men like Jervind live with the fear of being discovered as being assigned female at birth. That was the biggest threat to him in the incident at the massage parlour.

Jervind's telling of the masseuse's actions reminded me of a trans man friend's experience. He also had a masseuse move her hands between his legs in an offer to sexually please him. He reacted with shock as he interpreted her action as being akin to sexual assault. His interpretation of that stemmed from her not asking him if that was what he wanted. Jervind did not refer to his experience at the massage parlour as a sexual assault, and neither did his friends. It would be considered an instance of sexual assault, though, if it was examined from the perspective of consent prior to any initiation of a sexual act. The female masseuse assumed he expected a sexual act, even though he never asked for it. Jervind said "no," but this was after she initiated the sexual act.

Sexual consent is an agreement to participate in a sexual activity and should be obtained before any initiation of said sexual activity. This was not the case for Jervind (nor my friend). However, this does not imply that the masseuse is a perpetrator of sexual assault. It is likely that she assumed what she did was acceptable, as it may have been a common experience for her. She may also be acting under the assumption that it was expected of her when working with a male client. Both she and Jervind could also be under the commonly held impression that men cannot be victims of sexual assault.

In an examination of attitudes towards male rape amongst British undergraduate students, it was found that, for male victims, men and women felt that a hypothetical female perpetrator was less worrisome than a hypothetical male perpetrator due to an inappropriate application of gender stereotypes which assume that men should enjoy sex with women, and that assault by a woman is less severe (Davies et al., 2006). Also at play is the stereotype that men should be available for any sexual activity, and therefore initiation of sex by a woman is something that is favourable and should not be refused (Davies et al., 2006). The rape of a man by a woman is sometimes regarded as the ultimate emasculation and is therefore not considered to be of consequence or serious in nature (Sivakumaran, 2005). Indeed, the rape of a male by a female may be dismissed by some as enjoyable or comical, whereas male victims assaulted by male perpetrators may be asked if they are gay as a result of the attack and face stigma (Wakelin & Long, 2003).

Myths about rape also perpetuate the belief that men cannot be raped, especially by women. It is probably because of the prevalence of such myths that Jervind and his friends did not perceive the incident at the massage parlour as a sexual assault. Also, his friends seemed to have normalised the fact that it is not uncommon for men to experience these kinds of sexual acts at massage parlours. Jervind seemed to have done so, too, when he told me he would have consented had he been "a man." It was quite a different experience for my friend where he is now afraid of this happening again and goes through great pains to ensure he will not experience unwanted sexual advances at massage parlours.

EXPERIENCING MASCULINITY

Jervind's and his friends' reaction to the massage parlour incident also affirms Flood's (2008, p. 342) findings that for men sexual activity is a path to masculine status. The link between sexual activity and achievement of masculine status is also evident in Miles's experiences in his friendships with other cisgender men. He said:

> So far I have interacted with cis men that know I am trans and I notice the difference between the weight of what I say versus another cis dude but very rare. Like if this individual has knowledge that I am trans like on a certain topic that we're discussing for example women then maybe they're not going to really listen to me as much as another cis dude.

Noting an overall sense of being dismissed when speaking with cis men, Miles said that this happens especially when the topic of discussion is about women. Miles knew that he had dated more women than the men he spoke to, and yet he was told that he did not have enough experience with women. He attributed this to the cis men knowing that he did not have the "genitalia" (as Miles put it). Blue reported the same experience where he found his cisgender male friends did not speak to him about their experiences with their girlfriends because he "won't understand."

Here, Flood's (2008, p. 342) argument that sexual activity is not just a path to masculine status but is also for other men as the audience becomes pertinent. By this count, men engage in heterosexual sexual activities not for their own fulfilment but for performing for other men. Sexual activity with women is as much to please other men as it is for themselves. Also, drawing from Miles's and Blue's experiences, heterosexual sex becomes the medium through which male bonding is enacted. Men's bonding with each other, thus, is very much within the accepted norms of masculinity. It was unclear if Miles thought his friends perceived his lack of "genitalia" as an indication of his lack of experience with sex or if it was his own perception. Nonetheless, this perception itself arises from the prevalent notion that sex is heterosexual and centred around the penis and a vagina, and the insertion of the penis into the vagina (Wolfe, 2018).

Feelings and Masculinity

Trans men evaluated what they know about men and masculinities against these discoveries about the prominent role played by (hetero)sexual prowess. While Blue, Dines, and Jervind experienced blossoming bromances with their cis male friends, others navigated the role of emotional detachment in male homosocial bonding. Jake explained to me that this was something that he had experienced with his brother while growing up. He told me about his relationship with his brother:

> One thing that I [always told] him is guys don't cry they just bleed. If you can play then don't cry. You're not supposed to cry which is what someone else told me in the playground and I just [relayed] that. [But] when I deal with my sisters [it's different]. [If] they fell [when playing] then I'm like okay now I'm [going to] take a plaster for you and stuff. Where else for my brother it's like this idiot boy.

Jake was the oldest of four siblings, with two younger sisters and a brother. He was raised to be a "good role model" to his younger siblings, and there were expectations of him to set examples for others because he was the oldest and not because he was considered a son in his family. Turning to others to learn about being a man, he once heard a man in the playground say, "Guys don't cry they just bleed," and that stuck with him. He said he resonated more with that man compared to women or girls at the playground. He carried with him this belief and was unaccommodating of his brother's displays of emotions while being kind when his sisters cried. Ironically, Jake did not take into consideration that women bleed during menstruation or that many women sometimes endure severe pain while menstruating.

For Jake, crying or displaying negative emotions signalled that he was "weak." He said:

> You're a guy you're not supposed to show your feelings. Logically it does not make sense. But when it comes to the situation, I tend to go into that mode because that is how I perceive masculine to be. I don't show my emotion as easily anymore as a guy because if I were to cry, or if I were to show my weakest point, I'm not masculine I'm just a weak boy.

Of note here was Jake's use of the word "boy." For him, crying was an act that infantilised. The use of words like "boy" or "baby" denies grown-up status and approval from others with doing gender properly (Schrock & Schwalbe, 2009, p. 281). For Jake, a man who cries is one who has failed to properly do masculinity. The manly way of dealing with emotions is to get over them and not to experience or express them. Assigning emotional expression as something feminine (and to be masculine is to not be feminine), emotional detachment establishes individual masculinity while maintaining gender hierarchies. It establishes men as being more powerful than women. Jake does this by assigning weakness to crying. Sharon Bird (1996, p. 126), in analysing male homosocial relationships, argues that hegemonic masculinity is maintained through not expressing excessive emotionality. The distinction separates the "boys from the girls" and the men who fit the hegemonic norm and those who do not, thus establishing a hierarchy of masculinities. For Jake, his sisters were allowed to cry and receive kindness from him in return, something neither he nor his brother were allowed. He was separating the boys from the girls in his family and signalling himself as male. I asked Jake if he still believed that "boys don't cry they bleed" and he told me he does not. Yet, he struggled to cry when he needed to and recognised that he felt pain by not allowing himself to cry. It was this realisation that made him question the ideas of masculinity imposed on him.

Women's Reactions to Trans Men's Masculinity

Competitiveness, especially for the attention of and access to women, is also a mark of male homosocial relations. This was one aspect of male homosocial interactions that the trans men expressed discomfort with. Jameel spoke about his experience at a former workplace which was in a very male-dominated field. He had just been assigned two new assistants, who happened to be female:

> When I was working with a company [previously] they hired two new girls under me. I was a logistics manager. [There was] a group of guys who are engineers in the other room trying to catcall and everything. You know the usual. The only thing I said to them [was] if you really want to cat-call them you have to go through me. Because one thing is I have to protect them.

When he told me about this incident, Jameel spoke about how he had used his position as male to call out acts of sexual harassment that he witnessed. Jameel had also experienced sexual harassment before he began transitioning. He would get cat-called on the street, and that made him feel not only unsafe but also ashamed about his body. The men doing the cat-calling at Jameel's place of work were asserting their masculine identities by demonstrating their distance from femininity—the feminine was clearly the other. Male homosocial relations use interpersonal violence to express and maintain hierarchies of power amongst men and between men and women (Flood, 2008). The cat-calling of the female staff asserts the men's dominance over the women and also establishes a pecking order amongst themselves. By challenging that, Jameel was effectively situating himself outside of that hierarchy. However, by establishing himself as the women's protector, he was also asserting a different kind of hierarchy—that he was dominant over the women. While calling out a certain kind of masculinity, Jameel inadvertently perpetuated another type of masculinity that served to maintain the power imbalances between the genders.

Trans men's interactions with cisgender men produced feelings of affirmation (that they were performing masculinity properly) arising from being accepted by them, yet they also experienced contradiction. Blue, Dines, and Jervind all expressed a smooth transition in their friendships with cisgender men where these men accepted their identities and began using their preferred pronouns. Their struggle in these friendships was due to them still being seen as feminine because their masculinity was measured based on sexual experiences with women. Though friendships with cisgender men helped trans men like Jervind to navigate uncomfortable sexual encounters like he had at the massage parlour, it also asserted to him the fact that he was not a "real" man, i.e. he lacked a penis. The difficulties of being a man were also evident to Jake and Jameel, who found that abiding by ideas of masculinity meant that they inadvertently perpetuated and maintained the same power structures that they wanted to resist. These experiences became compounded in their heterosexual interactions with women.

Experiencing Relationships with Women

Where homosocial relations refer to dynamics organising non-romantic same-sex interactions, heterosocial refers to dynamics organising non-sexual relations between members of the other sex. Trans men's interactions with the women in their lives—family members, friends, colleagues, and girlfriends—play a role in how they conceptualise and experience their masculine selves. Where homosocial environments maintain hegemonic masculinity, i.e. men's emotional detachment, competition, and sexual objectification of women, heterosocial environments challenge it. Removing the need for competition and allowing space for emotions and feelings, heterosocial environments can be spaces where trans men experience comfort.

However, these experiences can also lead to frustration arising from trans men experiencing a tension in their wanting to resist stereotypes

EXPERIENCING MASCULINITY

about masculinity and pressure from women to subscribe to these very stereotypes. Coming out as a man implies that there are now different sets of expectations placed on trans men. The most prominent of the expectations is cis women's need to be taken care of, especially financially. The trans men spoke to me about being out to their female friends pre-transition (but upon beginning to identify as men to their friends), where they were expected to pay the bills and/or protect the women (ostensibly from being preyed on by other men). Blue talked about having experienced this when he was in school. When he came out to his parents, they challenged his masculine presentation and were initially opposed to his decision to transition, insisting that he was their daughter. Upon transition, however, he noticed a difference in the way his mother behaved with him:

> My mom has never really talked to me about financial issues. Recently she asked me if she could borrow money from me. Before this she [would be concerned that I did not have enough money] but now she asks me if I have money and if I can help. I think now she feels safer somehow. When we go out she would be like *manja*.[3] And then she [expects] me to order food for her. She looks at me in a certain way like I can handle things by myself.

Happy that his mother accepted him as a man, Blue struggled to resolve the changes in her behaviour with him. Her expectation of him ordering her food and providing financial support (albeit as a loan) is Blue's mother's expectation of him as a man, and he has to take on the roles and responsibilities of a son. Her being *manja* with him—an act of feminine demureness—was an implicit indication to him to look after her now that he was a man. Blue said this caught him by surprise because he believed his mother to be an empowered woman. She had worked all her life and continued to have a job in a high-powered position; she took charge of the family and was respected in her community.

The expectation of being looked after, especially financially, was something that Gene also experienced with his girlfriend:

> When we started dating she wanted me to pay for everything. And then I was like I thought you are a feminist. And she said yeah but I have this too you know. And I'm like that is so inconsistent you know. She said I'm

---

3   Manja is the Malay word to refer to child-like or coy behaviour exhibited by especially women when interacting with men.

not that kind of feminist. That is inconsistent. Don't go telling me you're a feminist that you want gender equality and then tell me actually I wish you would pay.

Unlike Blue's mother, Gene's girlfriend expressed a feminist ideology and a belief in gender equality that had him assuming that she believed in being an independent and autonomous woman. He expected his relationship to be different from his parents', which he described as traditional (see chapter 4). The contradictions between her beliefs and expectations of being looked after by him signalled to Gene her refusal to abide by stereotyped ideas of femininity but still expected him to fulfil stereotyped expectations of masculinity. He likened her feminist practice as "your money is my money; and my money is my money." He could not see their relationship as being equal if it was almost always on her terms.

Blue's mother and Gene's girlfriend exhibit benevolent sexism—a set of interrelated attitudes toward women that are sexist in terms of viewing women stereotypically and in restricted roles but that are subjectively positive in feeling and tone (for the perceiver) and tend to elicit behaviours typically categorised as prosocial (e.g. helping) or intimacy seeking (e.g. self-disclosure) (Glick & Fiske, 1996, p. 491). Sexism, though often exhibited through hostility toward women, can also manifest in subjective positive feelings towards women along with a sexist antipathy. Hence, a person (mostly men) may express the belief that women and men are not equal and yet respect women for bearing and raising children and claim to love women.

In unpacking the complexity of sexism, Peter Glick and Susan Fiske (1996) identify two components of sexism: benevolent sexism and hostile sexism, where the latter refers to what is recognised as prejudice against women. Benevolent sexism is not positive, as its underlying assumptions and bases are traditional stereotyping and masculine dominance (c.g. the man as the provider and the woman as his dependent). Extending the ideas of benevolent and hostile sexism to system justification theory (SJT) (Jost & Banaji, 1994) allows benevolent sexism to be seen as a particularly insidious form of prejudice, which women may find very positive and difficult to resist. Benevolent sexism is rewarding and extends to women the privilege of protection and chivalry (i.e. men opening doors for them and paying the bills). Studies have shown that women tend to profess a higher endorsement of benevolent sexism where there is a high national endorsement of sexist attitudes (Glick & Fiske, 1996, p. 491) and where there is internalisation of sexist attitudes (Becker, 2010). It is possible that Blue's mother and Gene's girlfriend both endorsed ideas of benevolent sexism as Malaysia meets

EXPERIENCING MASCULINITY

the standards of high national endorsement of sexist attitudes and their cultural internalisation.

Trans men come to encounter women's endorsement of benevolent sexism in different ways. Jervind's female friends expected him and his other male friends to make all the arrangements when they travelled together. His female friends expected him and his other male friends to accompany them shopping to carry their bags. Damon, whose mother had experienced domestic violence with his father, was surprised to find his mother expected him to play a more dominating role in his relationship with his girlfriend. Like Jervind's female friends, she also expected him to carry her shopping bags. Dines, however, had a different experience with his partner. He said about her:

> My partner is the type [who] likes everything [to be] equal. She has a very prejudice[d] view on men overall. That's why on certain occasions she will say don't behave like a typical man. But she addresses me as a man. She said you are a man okay? But you have that feminine aspect in you. So in terms of I can relate to her I can understand her better. So that's why if I derail from being equal she reminds me to get back on an equal platform.

When they met, Dines had just begun transitioning. As they worked together, she knew that he was assigned female at birth and learnt about being transgender and using the correct pronouns with him. Dines explained that his girlfriend was very conscientious about him not exhibiting what she thought were stereotypical masculine behaviours due to her history of bad romantic relationships. She believed in equality between men and women and dedicated time to communicate with Dines her expectations and what she would contribute to create an equal relationship for the both of them. Dines identified that an important aspect of their relationship was their ability to communicate with each other when they felt the other person had unfair expectations of them.

Unlike the women discussed earlier, Dines's partner did not seem to endorse or practice benevolent sexism. Evidence indicates that women who feel powerful, where they can experience more agency, are less likely to endorse benevolent sexism (Vial & Napier, 2017). It is possible that Dines's partner had come to experience a lot of personal power in her life, thus allowing her to question the need for benevolent sexism. This then allowed her to dismantle benevolent sexism in her relationship with Dines.

Gender Gatekeeping and Masculinity

When probed, Dines said that his girlfriend appreciated his sensitivity. He and his girlfriend had coded it as his "feminine aspect." The sensitivity was attributed to him being a good listener and (unlike Jake) not holding back when he felt the need to cry. His partner viewed his sensitivity in a positive light and saw it as an advantage in their relationship. Dines's former girlfriends had ended their relationship with him because "they said that you're not a full man. So no matter how much you try you can't be a man." While they also appreciated his sensitivity, like Jervind and Miles, Dines was thought to be inadequate as a partner because he had neither male reproductive organs nor a penis. His former girlfriends had moved on to relationships with cisgender men and gotten married and started families. Dines recognised that as a trans man he is unable to impregnate a woman. As Malaysian law does not yet allow legal gender recognition, he would be unable to get married, thus limiting the prospects of his romantic relationships.

While biological factors and systemic gender discrimination hinder Malaysian trans men's right to marriage and a family, there is also the role that women play in gatekeeping gender, which in turn affects trans men. Jervind experienced this at work where his female colleague insisted on outing him:

> My colleague always say[s] moreover you're still a girl. She mentions that purposely. When [a new person joins the team] the first thing she says is you *tahu dia perempuan ah*?[4]

Alexis identified as bisexual but has yet to date a woman. He told me:

> I have not dated any women. It's like in Malaysia I feel like I am too feminine for a lot of the women who are interested in guys. So I've not had the opportunity to date a woman. It's just the element of femininity. Like sure girls are like I like guys who are in touch with their emotions and that part of feminine side. But when it comes to other kinds of feminine expression. It's not really something they like.

The experiences of Dines, Jervind, and Alexis point to how trans men are viewed as women; they are deemed women and cannot be men because

---

4   Malay for, "Do you know this is a woman?"

they lack a penis (Schilt & Westbrook, 2015). In most cases, the trans man is seen as a masculine female who, according to Halberstam (1998, p. 9), is "vilified by heterosexist and feminist/womanist programs alike" as "female masculinity is generally received by hetero- and homo-normative cultures as a pathological sign of misidentification and maladjustment, as a longing to be and to have a power that is always just out of reach." In Alexis's case, women did not find him attractive as he was deemed "too feminine." As Alexis was assigned female at birth, he was smaller in size compared to the average Malaysian cis man. Hence, he may be deemed less attractive by women because of this. The trans man, therefore, is a woman who wants to be a man—a wannabe—"not a full man" in Dines's case, and one who needs to be called out and reminded of his place, as in Jervind's case.

Jervind's colleague outing him to other colleagues was her way of punishing him for not performing femininity in a socially expected way. Like masculinity, femininity is also ordered in a hierarchy where hegemonic femininity "consists of the characteristics defined as womanly that establish and legitimate a hierarchical and complementary relationship to hegemonic masculinity and that, by doing so, guarantee the dominant position of men and the subordination of women" (Schippers, 2007, p. 94). Hegemonic femininity is exalted into a position of superiority over other kinds of femininity to maintain the gender order upholding male domination. Attributes associated with masculinity, i.e. physical strength and male physical characteristics, must be unavailable to women to legitimise male superiority and social dominance over women. Women who are seen to exhibit these characteristics must be labelled as deviant and stigmatised; they must be punished for their transgression. Such femininities are deemed as contaminating to the social gender order, which Mimi Schippers (2007) aptly refers to as pariah femininities.

Gender (In)Equality and Masculinity

Expectations of femininity grant women privilege in that they may be placed on a pedestal (women are valued for their child-bearing abilities) or gain social currency from being able to ask for or get help, or from being warm and nice to people. As I discussed in chapter 3 (and in Jervind's experience highlighted above), women are disciplined for not performing femininity in socially acceptable ways. Thus, for "benevolent sexism" to be challenged, all notions of gender stereotypes and expectations would have to be challenged. Benevolent sexism sits alongside hostile sexism, which is the type that is most familiar to society, resulting in discrimination and violence against women. Men are more likely to endorse hostile sexism, while both men and women are likely to endorse benevolent sexism. Just as important, however, is that men who endorse hostile sexism may not endorse benevolent sexism, but men who endorse benevolent sexism may also endorse hostile sexism (Glick & Fiske, 1996). Since the endorsement of benevolent sexism plays a big role in perpetuating global gender inequalities and inequities, gender inequality in society must contend with challenging the privileges granted to women through it.

One of the difficulties in dealing with benevolent sexism is addressing violence against women. In chapter 3, I detailed the social and political conditions which make women vulnerable to violence. Yet, ironically, the global call for protection of women to curb the violence feeds into the ideas of benevolent sexism as women are seen as requiring protection—from men, from the law, from the state. These narratives of women as inherently vulnerable and in need of protection reproduce gender inequality (Westbrook & Schilt, 2014). Second-wave feminism constructed the identity of "woman" as that based on injury; collectively, women identify as having had experiences of gender-based violence (Phipps, 2021). The history of the women's movement in Malaysia was based on violence against women as it was seen by feminists to have the potential to unify women across class, geographic locations, cultures, and religions (Ng et al., 2006, p. 43).

The trans men I spoke to had come to recognise their relationship with women as bound by factors pertaining to violence against women and their perceived safety. Mitch told me about how he has learnt to be sensitive around women he did not know:

> Sometimes my partner has to tell me you're frightening the woman. Because you know sometimes [it's] so normal *blasa kun*[5]. Hello. How are you [Mitch enacts being physically close]? So the woman's like [Mitch enacts body in a stiff manner] like that. Sometimes it doesn't cross my mind because we're so used to it. My partner is like just don't do that anymore to women. Especially women that you don't know. I said why. They feel uncomfortable. Don't you see how uncomfortable she looks? Oh sorry. Okay. And then I realised that.

Mitch and others like Shane, Blue, and Miles told me that since they had transitioned, they notice that women behave differently around them. Shane

---

5   Malay for "normal, right?".

noticed that his female friends were less likely to hug him. Blue noticed that women who entered the train carriage he was on would rather stand than sit next to him. Miles noticed how women's bodies stiffened when he was close to them. These men recognised that it was because women have experienced sexual harassment or other kinds of inappropriate behaviour or violence from men in public spaces that they have learnt to be cautious. They also recognised that this may be a reason they faced scrutiny when they entered women's toilets before transitioning (as I discussed in chapter 4). Just as important in this aspect of their decision-making process was their own experiences of gender-based violence pre-transition; as Ben said, "I know what that's like. Just don't do that to women."

However, this same fear of violence from men has also led to movements around the world that legitimate discrimination against transgender women. Globally, the social construction of women as vulnerable and requiring protection from men has resulted in legislation that prohibits trans women from using women-only spaces (bathrooms, changing rooms) (Westbrook & Schilt, 2014). Transgender people's narratives and articulations of human rights documents, such as the Yogyakarta Principles, have made strong claims favouring the position of self-determination in decisions on transitioning; there should not be an imposition on the ways in which transgender people transition. The arguments arising from the protectionism-favouring feminists insisting that trans women are not women (and that trans men are women) have favoured legislations insisting that transgender people undergo surgeries to remove the penis in order to be recognised as women and to undergo hysterectomies in order to be recognised as male (Westbrook & Schilt, 2014).

The imposition of such standards and expectations on transgender people brings the conversation on gender back to genitals and reproductive organs. It also bases the anti-trans rhetoric on the argument that trans women cannot be considered women because they did not experience the "subordination" faced by women and girls (Zanghellini, 2020, p. 2). This kind of perspective lends to the view that oppression faced by cisgender women and girls makes them deserving of special status. This special status calls for women to be placed on a pedestal and afforded privileges in the form of protection from others, especially men.

The oppression and violence that trans women experience does not factor into these discussions and discounts the ways in which sex and gender intersect with cis and trans statuses. These intersections highlight the more complex and shifting contexts on which power is dependent rather than that captured by the male-female binary perspective. To adequately address gender-based violence, it would be necessary to think about and conceptualise violence in society beyond the binary structure of sex and gender or only from the perspectives of cisgender men and women.

It would be necessary to consider that, while women are predominantly the victims of gender-based violence, women can also be the perpetrators of violence. Subjecting transgender people to discrimination, whether barring trans women entrance into women-only spaces, insisting that trans men are women, or subjecting masculine-looking women and pre-transition trans men to the indignity of being policed in women's bathrooms, are forms of gender-based violence. Furthermore, these acts are harmful and perpetuate gender inequality and inequity. To fully address the issue of gender inequality, a more critical examination of women's role in perpetuating it (either by endorsing benevolent sexism or by perpetrating violence against trans women), is essential. The changes required are not just reforms of law but also inter- and intrapersonal changes that examine the role of benevolent sexism in our everyday lives.

In chapter 4, I discussed masculinity as a heuristic and its impact on trans men's cognitions in their development as men. It stands to reason that femininity could also be a heuristic, but femininity has not yet been examined critically (Schippers, 2007) to unpack its complex constructions. Since masculinity has always been seen as the source of discrimination and violence against women (Flood, 2008), there has not been a need to examine femininity. Femininity must be critically examined to fully understand the myriad ways that the gender binary (rather than masculinity) perpetuates gender inequality (Glick & Fiske, 1996). The women in trans men's lives affect their decision-making about masculinities as they have expectations of the trans men to maintain certain stereotyped ideas of masculinity while also expecting them to challenge stereotypes of femininity.

Trans men experience masculinity in homosocial and heterosocial spaces. While the trans men experience acceptance from cisgender men, they recognise that they may not fully fit in as they are still seen as "not fully men" owing, in no small part, to the fact that they do not have penises and are seen to lack sexual experience (perceived as legitimate only if it is between a penis and a vagina). Benevolent sexism plays a role in maintaining certain unequal gender dynamics between men and women, requiring a more critical examination of the social construction of femininity that problematises women as victims needing protection. In expressing disdain for hostile sexism, trans men make decisions about masculinity to ensure they are not perpetuating negative bias against women. In part 3 (chapters 6 and 7), I will provide an in-depth exploration of this link.

References

Becker, J. C. (2010). Why do women endorse hostile and benevolent sexism? The role of salient female subtypes and internalisation of sexist contents. *Sex Roles, 62*(7–8), 453–467. https://doi.org/10.1007/s11199-009-9707-4

Bird, S. R. (1996). Welcome to the men's club: Homosociality and the maintenance of hegemonic masculinity. *Gender & Society, 10*(2), 120–132. https://doi.org/10.1177/089124396010002002

Connell, R. (2005). *Masculinities* (2nd edition). Polity Press.

Davies, M., Pollard, P., & Archer, J. (2006). Effects of perpetrator gender and victim sexuality on blame towards male victims of sexual assault. *The Journal of Social Psychology, 146*(3), 275–291. https://doi.org/10.3200/SOCP.146.3.275-291

DeAngelis, M. (2014). *Reading the bromance: Homosocial relationships in film and television*. Wayne State University Press.

Flood, M. (2008). Men, sex and homosociality: How bonds between men shape their sexual relations with women. *Men and Masculinities, 10*(3), 339–359. https://doi.org/10.1177/1097184X06287761

Glick, P., & Fiske, S. (1996). The ambivalent sexism inventory: Differentiating hostile and benevolent sexism. *Journal of Personality and Social Psychology, 70*(39), 491–592. https://doi.org/10.1037/0022-3514.70.3.491

Halberstam, J. (1998). *Female masculinity*. Duke University Press.

Jost, J. T., & Banaji, M. R. (1994). The role of stereotyping in system-justification and the production of false consciousness. *British Journal of Social Psychology, 33*, 1–27. https://doi.org/10.1111/j.2044-8309.1994.tb01008.x

McDiarmid, E., Gill, P. R., McLachlan, A., & Ali, L. (2017). "That whole macho male persona thing": The role of insults in young Australian male friendships. *Psychology of Men and Masculinities, 18*(4), 352–360. https://doi.org/10.1037/men0000065

Ng, C., Mohamad, M., & Tan, B. H. (2007). *Feminism and the women's movement in Malaysia: An unsung (r)evolution*. Routledge.

Phipps, A. (2021). White tears, white rage: Victimhood and (as) violence in mainstream feminism. *European Journal of Cultural Studies, 24*(1), 81–93. https://doi.org/10.1177/1367549420985852

Robinson, R., Anderson, E., & White, A. (2018). The bromance: Undergraduate male friendships and the expansion of contemporary homosocial boundaries. *Sex Roles, 78*(1–2), 94–106. https://doi.org/10.1007/s11199-017-0768-5

Schilt, K., & Westbrook, L. (2015). Bathroom battlegrounds and penis attacks. *Contexts, 14*(3), 26–31. https://doi.org/10.1177/1536504215596943

Schippers, M. (2007). Recovering the feminine other: Masculinity, femininity, and gender hegemony. *Theory and Society, 36*(1), 85–102. https://doi.org/10.1007/s11186-007-9022-4

Schrock, D., & Schwalbe, M. (2009). Men, masculinity and manhood acts. *Annual Review of Sociology, 35*(1), 277–295. https://doi.org/10.1146/annurev-soc-070308-115933

Sivakumaran, S. (2005). Male/male rape and the taint of homosexuality. *Human Rights Quarterly, 27*(4), 1274–1306.

Vial, A. C., & Napier, J. L. (2017). High power mindsets reduce gender identification and benevolent sexism among women (but not men). *Journal of Experimental Social Psychology, 68*, 162–170. https://doi.org/10.1016/j.jesp.2016.06.012

Westbrook, L., & Schilt, K. (2014). Doing gender determining gender: Transgender people, gender panics, and the maintenance of the sex/gender/sexuality system. *Gender & Society, 28*(1), 32–57. https://doi.org/10.1177/0891243213503203

Wakelin, A., & Long, K. (2003). Effects of victim gender and sexuality on attributions of blame to rape victims. *Sex Roles, 49*(9), 477–487. https://doi.org/10.1023/A:1025876522024

Wolfe, M. J. (2018). Materialising effects of difference in sex education: The 'absurd' banana penis. *Gender and Education, 30*(8), 1065–1077. https://doi.org/10.1080/09540253.2018.1451625

Zanghellini, A. (2020). Philosophical problems with the gender-critical feminist argument against trans-inclusion. *SAGE Open, 10*(2). https://doi.org/10.1177/2158244020927029

Part 3

I Know I Am a Man

6. Challenging Masculinity

Abstract: Analysis of 23 trans men's narratives indicate three distinct stages of decision-making. This chapter begins to explore how trans men, upon living as men, come to recognise male privilege that they begin to experience because they are men. Living as men brings them to challenge the idea of what being a man is as they contend that they may never be regarded as "real men" due to their biology, bringing their female histories to the fore. This brings them to question hegemonic masculinity, thus posing a challenge to it being a supposed ideal for men. The chapter also explores the intersections of trans identities, masculinities, and race in Malaysia.

Keywords: trans men, Malaysia, decision-making, race, gender relations

Living as men, and being privy to the myriad gendered relations with men and women, enable trans men to gain insights into the complexities of masculinities and manhood. Their experiences of being perceived as men-but-not-quite allow them to transgress spaces that they otherwise would not have had access to, allowing them glimpses of what may be unseen by cisgender people. From their interactions, they learn that trans men can escape the kinds of abuses and discrimination faced by trans women due to an implicit understanding that it is good to aspire to manhood and not to be a woman. This outsider-within (Collins, 1986, p. S27) perspective enables, for example, unique insights into the changes in gender relations that enable male privilege. They know they have not changed, but the change in gender identity avails them of a host of options and opportunities that were denied them before, when they were perceived as women.

These insights allow for the understanding of the role of gender stereotypes in maintaining structures of inequality. Challenging the notion that women can make gains in the workplace by making different decisions on education, working styles, or division of labour at home, Kristen Schilt (2006, p. 469) argues that gender inequality in the workplace is due to co-workers and employers' reliance on gender stereotypes to evaluate men's and

---

Kumaresan, Vizla. *Trans Men in Malaysia: Decision-Making, Masculinity and Manhood.* Amsterdam: Amsterdam University Press, 2025.
DOI: 10.5117/9789048562596_CH06

women's achievements and skills. Trans men challenge such stereotypes of masculinity in their process of becoming men and experience a difference in personal and public interactions upon transitioning, through which they get to witness first-hand how male privilege works. This impacts their decision-making on masculinity, allowing them to move beyond utilising masculinity as a heuristic and developing more complex decision-making strategies by taking into consideration their feelings towards their newfound access to male privilege and their aspirations for gender equality.

Experiencing Male Privilege

Privilege refers to the unearned benefits afforded to powerful social groups within systems of oppression (Case et al., 2012, p. 3) at the cost of groups with less power experiencing discrimination. Privilege is systemic: it is built and reinforced via institutions. Male privilege is one such system that provides benefits reinforced by male-centric social norms based on the patriarchal design and historical binary developed by and for men (Case et al., 2014, p. 723). The trans men told me that they began to experience this privilege in various ways as they transitioned. Damon spoke to me about his experience at a police station following an accident:

> Recently I got into an accident with my car. I was treated very much differently because no one knew I was female. [I had to reveal my identity card at the police station] I was very scared. But they were like circle the *laki*.[1] My official [documents identify me] as female. No choice. But he really [said] don't worry, boy.

The experience stood out for Damon because when he had gone to report an accident before transitioning, the police personnel at the station had first ignored him, and he waited for other people who came after him to be attended to. Then, the police implied that the accident was his fault because females are bad drivers. After transitioning, however, Damon said that the police did not stop to question if the accident was his fault. They spoke to him with a lot more respect than his previous experience and were even ready to overlook the fact that his identity documents indicated that he was assigned female. Damon added that his girlfriend and sister were with him, and they were also taken aback by how he was treated by the police.

---

1   Malay for male.

CHALLENGING MASCULINITY

They all concluded that Damon was receiving this treatment because he was now male. This experience also stood out for Damon as he was fully aware that the police are known to be hostile and oftentimes violent to transgender people.

Damon was assumed to be a better driver because he was male. Female drivers' experiences mirror women's social position: in societies with less gender equality, women drivers face worse discrimination or bias (Li & Luo, 2020). For instance, in many societies, women who drive are confined by gender bias in the form of patriarchal norms that discriminate against women and practices that hinder them from exercising the same rights as men in social life. When women step into public domains previously dominated by men, stereotypes based on conventional gender roles may follow, sometimes wearing the mask of patriarchal care. Such extra attention to women, sometimes presuming they are less competent than men, may be reflected in folklore, public policy, and media coverage (Li & Luo, 2020, p. 776). Thus, the stereotype of women as bad drivers is perpetuated and strengthened despite evidence that women drivers are as good as, and sometimes better than, male drivers.

Damon knew that becoming a better driver was not a side effect of transitioning; he drove the same way he did before. The difference now was that he was a man and, therefore, was perceived to be a better driver. It was an unfounded bias and was not lost on Damon. Even though Damon recognised this as a bias, he also saw that he was able to benefit from it. Other trans men recalled similar experiences of recognising bias based on how people responded to them. Hans told me about how he came to recognise it at his workplace:

> There was one time my manager was angry about something. So when a colleague of mine who is a female tried to say something it was quickly dismissed. But when I [spoke up] they listen[ed] to me. So a few of them kind of complained to me like *eh tengok kau cakap je dengar kita orang cakap tak nak dengar*[2] you know.

In recognising that the content of what he was saying was no different from that of his female colleagues, Hans acknowledged the power that his voice now carried. In doing so, he correctly identified that workers' performances are evaluated by gender; men are viewed as more competent than women workers; men's success is attributed to their abilities while women's success

---

2   Malay for, "Look how they listen when you say it but don't listen when we say it."

is often perceived as stemming from luck; and men are rewarded more than women for offering ideas and opinions and for taking on leadership roles in group settings (Schilt, 2006, p. 475). In recognising the unfairness of this privilege, Hans said that it "kinda made me feel bad for the women." Hans decided that he would use this privilege to become a conduit for the women; he became a medium for their ideas at work and was conscious of not taking credit for his female colleagues' ideas.

Male Privilege and the Pedestal Effect

While Hans's motivations are commendable, his actions are actually a strategy that lends him greater privilege as he may be perceived as having more authority in the workplace. Men who engage in these kinds of behaviours, while helpful and positive towards challenging dominant gender relations, gain more privilege as a result of the pedestal effect. The pedestal effect results in gratuitous acclaim, heightened attention, unearned credibility, and romantic attraction for the men (Peretz, 2020, p. 448). Such are the complexities of these gender relations that, even in feminist situations, male privilege persists. Challenging male privilege is limited in effect because of the structural nature of privilege itself. Even when challenged at an individual level, male privilege not only persists but perpetuates structurally.

The privileges pile on. Trans men who are out at their workplace report receiving advantages at work following their transition—gaining competency and authority, respect and recognition for hard work, body privilege, economic opportunities, and status (Schilt, 2006, p. 475). Hans felt this and said, "People just listen to you more." Kyle reported that the masculinising effect of testosterone on his face, especially, meant that he had less of a "baby face." The consequence of this was that people took him more seriously and regarded him as more competent. The change in authority is noticeable only because trans men often have experienced the reverse—being thought, on the basis of gender alone, as less competent workers who receive less authority from employers and coworkers (Schilt, 2006).

There seem to be exceptions to this experience, though. Cunie, who had his own construction business, experienced blatant disrespect from the cis men who worked for him. He attributed this to their knowing that he was assigned female at birth. Cunie had not gone through any medical transitioning but had socially transitioned. He has a preferred name and dressed in men's clothes. Some of the men who worked for him thought he was *pengkid* (discussion in chapter 2) and that he was acting (*berlagak*) like

CHALLENGING MASCULINITY

a man. The stark difference in authority between Cunie (who ran his own successful business) and the others is attributed to their perceived proximity to femininity. Cunie was still seen as female and, therefore, not worthy of respect or recognition despite his status as their employer, despite the fact that he was successful and good at his job.

Male Privilege and Women

The other element of male privilege that became clear to the trans men was the expectation that men are to have more power in their relationships with women and gain from women's labour. Damon told me about how his male cousins reacted to his relationship with his girlfriend:

> I feel like there is a patriarchy thing where it's like we are men. You are women (Damon moves his hands to indicate a separate category). And when my cousin brothers started seeing me as a boy [they say] let [the women] get up and do. It doesn't matter. [Tell] your girlfriend to get you a glass of water. It's ok I can go get it myself. I feel like we should be doing it instead of asking them, you know? Even my sister's boyfriend [tells her] you go get me breakfast. And she does it.

Damon continues to have a penchant for being suspicious about masculinity and male gender roles because of how his father had abused him, his mother, and his sisters. Therefore, he challenges ideas and stereotypes of masculinity from women and men. He referred to his cousins and sister's boyfriend as "typical men" who had ingrained ideas of gender roles and stereotypes, which he disagreed with. They believed that they should benefit from women's labour because they are men, and relied on homosocial environments to socialise masculinity. It is also in these kinds of environments that male privilege is maintained. Bob Pease (2016, p. 51) states:

> [I]t is important to differentiate between the institutionalised patriarchal system, which refers to the structural advantages and privileges that men enjoy, and the personal patriarchal system which involves men's face-to-face interactions with women both at home and in the public sphere. Because all men are socialised within patriarchy, they will have all received cultural messages that they have a right to make normative claims upon women. These claims include deferential treatment, unpaid domestic labour and child care, sexual services and emotional support.

Aside from socialisation being a way for people to learn about how to be men or women, it is also about learning the subtle (and not so subtle) aspect of power between genders—that men are superior to or have more power than women, and that this difference should be made evident in interpersonal social interactions. It is legitimated by the institutional power of culture, family, and other social structures. Damon saw the role that was played by his family in maintaining this idea as his sister did not see how he treated his girlfriend as something that could be possible for her. She told him that it was not how she was raised. The power of that socialisation was strong enough that his sister would not question the gender structure she found herself in, nor could she imagine another way of being. What baffled Damon even more was that she refused to question it despite having witnessed how it negatively affected their mother. Furthering his point on men feeling entitled to women's labour, Pease (2016, p. 51) says:

> Many men thus come to believe that they deserve something from women which they then experience as an entitlement. The totality of these entitlements and claims are what constitute male privilege. This sense of entitlement may not necessarily be conscious and it may only come into their awareness when they are deprived of this unreciprocated service. On such occasions, it may result in physical violence as a form of control.

The entitlement that Damon's cousins felt was theirs, and should be Damon's, was their girlfriends or wives providing them care in the form of getting them a glass of water or in other forms of labour. Damon witnessed how it was his mother's duty to make sure the meals were prepared for his father, and that these should be ready as soon as he sat at the table. He hated this about his father and thought it was unfair to his mother. Damon saw it all as part of the violence that his father used to control his mother, sisters, and himself.

While Damon was quick to call out his cousins' behaviours, or even his sister when she reprimanded him for challenging these gender stereotypes, it came at a cost. His sister thought he was strange, and his cousins and other men questioned his masculinity. Damon often got asked if he was a gay man:

> This is how you have to be to be perceived as a man. Behave like an ass then you get whatever you desire. You feel like everyone is going to accept you. I still feel like no one is going to accept me because I feel like I am coming off as a gay man. You look like a man but you are coming off very much like a gay man, very soft as a man. I was hit with that question just maybe two [or] three weeks ago. I was like well I have a girlfriend so you can't call me gay.

CHALLENGING MASCULINITY

Damon was perceived as gay because he was "soft" and "nice"; features typically associated with the feminine, thus subordinating masculinity. Connell (1995, p. 78) states that in contemporary European or American society, there is a dominance of heterosexual men and the subordination of homosexual men through the cultural stigmatisation of gay identities and through abuse and legal violence. This is true not only for European or American society but also for Malaysian society. The Malaysian Penal Code (Act 574, p. 209) still carries section 377 pertaining to "sex against the order of nature," with section 377A pertaining to anal and oral sex. While this provision does not directly criminalise gay men, it has been recognised as one that particularly targets homosexuality (Shah, 2018, p. 233). Connell (2005, p. 78) argues that patriarchy views gayness as imbued with whatever is symbolically expelled from hegemonic masculinity: items ranging from fastidious taste in home decoration to receptive anal pleasure. Being gay, therefore, is seen as a failure of doing or attaining masculinity (i.e. repudiating femininity) as it is seen to retain aspects of femininity. Hence, Damon's refusal to partake in these typically stereotyped masculine behaviours is his failing to be properly masculine.

Male Privilege and Men

White Lotus faced another challenge confronting these ideas of masculinity when he was entrusted by a cis male colleague to listen to his tales of infidelity. This male colleague was dating another colleague, and told White Lotus that he was also seeing other women. White Lotus decided to tell her about it. The male colleague then socially ostracised White Lotus for having violated the "bro code" supposedly existing between men:

> The other day I was talking to my good friend and I was telling her how being a male means that you really have to understand what the bro code is all about. And I really don't understand the bro code because all my life I have been around women.

Despite the "bro code" only recently becoming popular through the media, White Lotus assumed that it was a ubiquitous element of masculine culture. The women in his life, especially his mother, taught him to value things like being trustworthy, and being a man meant that trustworthiness was compromised. For Damon, being a man meant "being an ass." Similarly, Jameel told me that recognising that he had male privilege made him feel like "an asshole." For these three men, male privilege was a source of shame which fed an idea of what they should not be. For them, challenging notions such as the "bro code" was essential in ensuring women were safe in their relationships with men.

In discussing the role played by violence in maintaining gender relations, Pease (2016, p. 50) states that violence against women is a tool men use to locate themselves in relation to other men and reproduce, through their practices, a particular form of masculine self. Men demonstrate their manhood in relation to other men more than in relation to women. Men also use violence to establish and maintain a hierarchy amongst themselves, as many of the trans men came to discover. Damon was shoved and pushed in one of his encounters with his girlfriend's male colleagues, who expected him to retaliate. Damon did not retaliate and de-escalated the situation instead, which led to his girlfriend's colleague's remark about him being a nice guy and assuming he was gay (discussed above). The implication that Damon may be gay was to highlight a lack of masculinity.

For many of the trans men, the confrontation with the expectations to enact violence in order to be seen as masculine makes them question it. Shane lived in Australia for a time, where he said he learnt "everything that a man shouldn't be":

> That hyper aggression. There wasn't a day that I went out at night that I wouldn't see a bloody fight. The way that they treated one another was not with respect. And the way they talked about women or they treated women even though I felt then I wasn't in the privacy circle of male whatever I could tell that there was no respect there either. And for me it's always like yes as much as I like the country and I like the work but how people treat one another here is fucking bullshit. I never ever want to be like a man here.

Shane witnessed a particular kind of male friendship referred to as "mateship" in Australia (Towns & Terry, 2014, p. 1015), which privileges male homosocial bonding, male loyalty, and heterosexuality that permeates many aspects of life. While providing a sense of connection between men, mateship also carries negative elements, which include competition, status, hierarchy, loyalty, and homophobia. It privileges a culture of silence that makes it difficult to address the more damaging elements of masculine cultures and male violence in relationships, focusing instead on women's violence against men when faced with challenges to mateship culture.

When White Lotus disclosed his male colleague's infidelity, he disrupted the male bonding that is expected in homosocial interactions. As many men experience discomfort at the idea of challenging other men, the requirements and expectations of mateship discourage them from challenging their male friends, resulting in collusion with the violence their male friends perpetrate (Pease, 2016, p. 51). White Lotus's decision to challenge the "bro code" silence was him refusing to collude with the system of male privilege that enables violence in masculine culture. This refusal to collude was also evident in Shane's decision to not engage in that aspect of Australian male culture and also in deciding on the kind of masculinity he will come to portray.

For Hans, Damon, White Lotus, Jameel, and Shane, challenging and outright refusing male privilege is an essential element in their decision-making around their process of becoming men. When I set out to answer my research question, I had hoped to develop a cognitive model of this decision-making process. The data collection and analysis processes of my research led me to discover that there was more to the decision-making process than that of a computational model. Trans men were making decisions based on their own experiences—from experiencing the world as female, and also experiencing the world as male. Gender was not just being done to them; they were also actively doing something to gender. In this process, they exhibited intentionality, forethought, self-reactiveness, and self-reflectiveness, which are all core features of human agency (Bandura, 2001, p. 6–10). Intentionality is the ability to plan a future course of action and to work on it while being able to change the plan as it unfolds. Forethought refers to people's ability to do what is necessary to foresee life as a project that requires the reordering of priorities and the structuring of life in a manner to meet one's goals. Self-reactiveness is the ability to motivate oneself, make goals, and monitor them accordingly, which requires self-reflectiveness to examine oneself. In seeing their becoming men as a process, trans men exercise their agency in actively thinking about the kind of men they want to be, allowing them to question, subvert, and imagine new ways of being and doing masculinities.

Thus far, I have explored the role played by socialisation in the construction of the interviewees' masculinities. I examined the decision-making of trans men based on their experiences of masculinity through social relations—with other men and also women. In the next section, I explore the role played by the state in affecting how trans men make decisions about their masculinity and also their process of becoming men.

Challenging Hegemonic Masculinity

The issues of, and surrounding, race and religion in Malaysia are complex. Unpacking the intersections of race, religion, and masculinity problematises the notions of power in Connell's concept of hegemonic masculinity. Trans men's narratives demonstrated that Connell's concept of hegemonic masculinity resonates in Malaysia but diverges from the realities of gender relations in the country when viewed from its specificities of race relations. The trans men interviewed for this project consist of a mix of Malay (7), Chinese (9), and Indian (6) Malaysians. One of the trans men identified as Chindian, which is a Malaysian word that denotes being of mixed parentage—Chinese and Indian. However, there is no recognised category of Chindian; the trans man who identified himself to me as such said that he marked the category "Other" when filling in forms.

Race in Malaysia is highly contested, and debate also extends to the appropriate language required to unpack its complexities. The use of the word "race" demonstrates how people in Malaysia have been racialised through various state processes (Mandal, 2004, p. 57). Gender, too, has been constructed through similar state processes and intersects to affect gender relations in Malaysia. Historically, class was used as a means of social control and manipulation, which resulted in the belief that race was more meaningful in explaining social conflict in Malaysia (Abraham, 2004, p. 12). Each of the racial groups (Malay, Chinese, Indian) has its own history of how social class became subsumed by race. For instance, the British segregated communities according to labour, i.e. Malays in agriculture, Chinese in business, and Indians in plantations. Expanding on this, Sharmani P. Gabriel (2015, p. 783) says:

> Race is a fundamental organizing principle in Malaysian society. Founded on the political economy of British colonial rule in the nineteenth century, it continues to be used in the post-colonial imagining of the nation and its identity. It is ascendant over other markers such as class, gender and religion and remains the most readily referenced signifier of difference in Malaysia. Written into public policies and practices and embedded into the formal structures and institutions of state, race is a ubiquitous term in the public lexicon, from parliament and lecture theatres to everyday domains of exchange.

More than any other identity marker, race in Malaysia has the potential to impact people's access to services or education as it is the basis of many public policies related to these issues. It is common for anyone to be asked, "What are you?" to ascertain their race. It is an identity that is ascribed and remains static; in Malaysia, it is stated in a person's birth certificate and is an identity marker that cannot be changed. This is contrary to ideas of race scholars like Stuart Hall (1990, p. 394), whose understanding of race is that it is a construct produced from historical and material factors of society where race is a matter of "becoming" as well as "being"; it changes in experience and expression depending on history, culture, and power.

The British introduced the concept of "race" in its Malay colonies, defining who is a "Malay" in order to form separations between the indigenous population and the Chinese and Indian immigrants (Shah, 2018, p. 105). It is argued that Malaysian social policies continue the legacies of the former British colonial masters of "divide and rule." Upon Malaysia's independence in 1957, the British left intact racial, religious, and tribal animosities which they themselves created and fostered during colonial rule (Shah, 2018, p. 109). The history of race in Malaysia is rooted in colonialism. Race as a social category is often used as a convenient excuse for the postcolonial Malaysia project to continue its use to maintain structures of power and social divisions that have spillover effects on aspects such as gender and sexuality. Rao (2020, p. 10) states that these structures of power and social divisions impact queers' postcolonial "presents" as they are marked by the past and future, where there are different resources and struggles. Malaysian transgender people's selves and identities are a point of contestation between the precolonial period, where there was reported to be a high level of acceptance, and the postcolonial experience of being labelled products of "Western culture."

While Malaysia boasts a multicultural and multifaith tradition, Islam has an exalted position in the country. The Malaysian Federal Constitution states that "Islam is the religion of the Federation," and it connects to race by defining a "Malay" as a person "who professes the religion of Islam." Malaysia's political history has seen the interests of the Malay people (hence, Muslim) prioritised; the politics of Malay leaders has centred around goals of achieving Malaysian-Malay success over others (Goh, 2014, p. 604). The state has a close relationship with Islam, and has invested in strengthening Islamic institutions in the country. For instance, the Department of Islamic Development (JAKIM) was established in 1997 and is responsible for the administration of Islamic affairs in the country. The budget allocation for JAKIM has shown a steady increase from RM1.4 billion in 2021 to RM1.9 billion in 2023 (Yuen, 2019; Tee, 2020; Musa, 2024).

Amongst its duties in handling matters of Islamic concern, JAKIM manages a conversion therapy programme aimed at LGBTQ Muslims. The state, and powers related to it, are closely tied with the Malay and Muslim identities, thus regulating gender identities and sexualities. Though its powers are limited to people identifying as Muslim, the standards and practices of JAKIM, along with the Islamic perspective in Malaysia, create an overall culture that affects the lives of non-Muslim people in Malaysia. The dominant Islamic narrative intersects with trans men's masculinity and their own racial/cultural milieu.

Race and the Construction of Gender Relations in Malaysia

Gene spoke of the role of Chinese culture in his masculinity. He was critical of the privileges he perceived are granted to men, such as those his father received in his home. Ben, too, spoke about the Chinese cultural expectations of masculinity that he was raised with: "Well they're really old school and outdated like the guy has to be the sole breadwinner of the family [and] he has to be taller [and] has to be older than the female." Ben was raised with specific stereotypes of masculinity, which he said were rooted in his cultural background. Although he rejects these ideas, these stereotypes are espoused by his brother and parents, who run and manage their family and household based on these beliefs. Expectations of being the sole breadwinner are not necessarily limited to Chinese masculinity. Division of labour is a prominent aspect of gender relations where masculinity has been associated with the public realm and femininity with the private. However, in Asian cultures that value hierarchy—such as in the Chinese culture—the male sole breadwinner is seen to confer respect, power, and authority in the family. Traditional Chinese culture identifies two main streams of masculinity: the scholarly, intellectual, gentle-mannered *wén* type or the physical, action-oriented, bold, and forceful *wu* type (Jankowiak & Xuan, 2014, p. 5). These two types of masculinity do not exist in an either/ or relation, but rather have different values depending on the social-political situation of the time.

Elements of the local culture influence the values of masculinity that men are expected to aspire to. In Confucianism-influenced Singapore, for example, a gentleman (*junzi* 君子) is a person who is cultivated and possesses the five basic Confucian virtues of humanity (*ren* 仁), righteousness (*yi* 义), loyalty (*zhong* 忠), propriety (*li* 礼), and filial piety (*xiao* 孝). The gentleman is expected to know and observe the relationship and correct behaviour between superiors and inferiors, among friends, kinspeople, strangers, and enemies. His understanding of the teachings and his proper observations will, therefore, result in stability within the family, society, and state (Eng, 2018, p. 17).

Regardless of the type of masculinity that is preferred, femininity is viewed as inferior due to the perception that females are less capable of controlling their emotions and less effective managers of their own lives. There is a social preference for *wén* masculinity, especially when it comes to issues of dating, marital relationships, and interactions among colleagues where mild manners are valued. However, homosocial relations among men can also be violent, sexually charged, and competitive. The focus is on the consumption of alcohol, the use of crude language, vulgar displays, being sexually insensitive, engaging in overtly competitive status assertions, materialistic displays of self-importance, and sexually flirtatious encounters are played out through camaraderie to establish male solidarity. These homosocial relations require the embracing of *wu* masculinity (Jankowiak & Xuan, 2014, p. 5). These aspects of masculinity are relatively similar to European/American cultural norms. There are some universal aspects of masculinity, though these may be experienced locally within one's context of ethnicity or nationality. The core feature seems to be the superiority of the masculine (read: male and man) and the inferiority of the feminine (read: female and woman).

This is also prevalent in the way Indian Malaysian trans men describe their racialised experiences of masculinity. Damon spoke of the patriarchal strain he notices amongst Indian men in his life. LaudeB said that his experience of Indian masculinity was being "crude and loud." Indians in Malaysia have a varied history of migration, but the most common was labour migration during the colonial period. Indians were brought to colonial Malaya primarily to work the plantations. The oppressive environments under which Indian labourers lived and worked have been previously documented (Abraham, 2004). Ron Backus (2017) draws parallels between the discrimination faced by the darker-skinned Indians and that of Black people, thus describing systemic racism against Indians in Malaysia. The stereotype of the hyperaggressive and hypersexualised Black man is also imposed on Indian men, who constitute subordinated masculinity in the heteropatriarchal sense. These Indian men utilise hyper-masculine counter strategies in dealing with everyday experiences of racism. Like Damon, Ben, and Gene, LaudeB does not subscribe to these ideas of masculinity.

While these Malaysian trans men have espoused rejection of these elements of race-based perceptions of masculinity, it does govern some aspects of their interactions with others. Liw, who identifies as Chinese, paid close attention to the subtle differences he noticed in how men interact with others. "Malay guys only shake hand[s] [with] guys not women." Liw took note of this social norm and used it to help him pass as a man. Knowing how to manage interactions with Malay men allowed Liw to escape from scrutiny regarding his masculine gender expression. Shaking hands with a Malay woman violates social mores where it is not uncommon in Malaysia for men and women to not only be segregated in certain spaces, but also for physical interaction with each other to be limited. It is assumed that state powers can govern interactions between men and women. For instance, the state[3] of Kelantan has banned cinemas since 1990 when the religiously conservative Parti Islam Se-Malaysia (PAS) replaced the coalition government Barisan Nasional (National Front) (BN). The ban was imposed as cinemas were deemed to pave the way for "social ills" (Bernama, 2019), with "social ills" referring to illicit sexual acts between men and women. Hence, interactions between men and women also bear a moral weight in Malaysian society. *Zina*—illicit heterosexual sex—is a crime under the Shariah Criminal Offences Act (SCOA) and is punishable by imprisonment, whipping, a fine, or any combination of the three (Shah, 2018, p. 230).

Issues of morality are not limited to relationships between the sexes. Personal morality is also a consideration, especially for Muslims. Malaysian law requires Muslim men to attend Friday prayers at designated mosques and to fast during Ramadan, and prohibits drinking and gambling (Moustaffa, 2018, p. 31). While some prayers are done at home, the afternoon prayer, especially on Fridays, is undertaken in congregation at the mosque which is a gendered space; men and women are separated, and prayers are usually led by men (Mahaveera & Hamid, 2017). Ani Zonneveld, a Malaysian female imam in Los Angeles, faced criticism and censure when attempting to lead prayers; she was chided for doing a "man's job," even when she was not leading prayers in Malaysia. The minister for religious affairs had to issue a statement announcing that missing three consecutive Friday prayers was permissible during the Covid-19 pandemic, when the Malaysian government had imposed various restrictions on physical movement and gathering of people (Bernama, 3 April 2020). The state, therefore, has great influence on Muslims fulfilling their prayer obligations—both their fulfilment and how they are done. Mitch felt

---

3   The Federation of Malaysia is made up of 13 states (11 in Peninsular/West Malaysia and two in East Malaysia) and two federal territories.

CHALLENGING MASCULINITY

this pressure to fulfil his religious obligations from the Muslim men in his community. He said:

> [We had] this *orang Masjid*[4] [who] came to the house. Asked me why I never come to the *masjid*. You know as a Malay community *sembahyang*.[5] I [said] okay. When I want to come I will come la.

It is not uncommon in Malaysia for (especially) Malay men to comment on the behaviours of other Muslims as a form of social moral policing. Women experience *tegur*[6] regarding their clothing—if they dress immodestly, or even if they are deemed to be wearing a hijab that is of insufficient length. This can happen in real-life situations or online interactions. Men, too, experience *tegur*, but with regard to their attendance at congregational prayers. It is considered rude to retort to this exhortation of being a good Muslim, especially for women. Women who challenge such comments are threatened with violence, especially rape, or are called bad Muslim women for being dismissive of advice that is meant for their own good. Mitch, however, managed to inform, without censure, the person from the community mosque that he would attend prayers should he wish to. Mitch explained to me that he does not conform to the pressures from society, and he saw his refusal to participate in congregational prayer as an extension of that aspect of his personality. Mitch believes that religion is a personal matter, and he practices his faith in a way that feels appropriate to him. Mitch did note that, while his decision was respected by the people from the mosque, women who refuse men's *tegur* would face violent repercussions.

Mitch's partner is non-Muslim, and they raise two children together. In Malaysian law, a non-Muslim wishing to marry a person of Muslim faith must convert to Islam (Moustaffa, 2018, p. 31). Legal gender recognition is not available in Malaysia (APTN, 2017), and the country's laws do not recognise same-sex marriage.[7] As Mitch was assigned female at birth, his identity documents denote him as female. Being the oldest trans man amongst those interviewed for this study, he had been living as a man for more than 20 years. Referring to his partner as his wife, he describes their relationship as

---

4   People from the mosque.
5   Malay word for pray.
6   Malay word for reprimand.
7   The various states' Shariah Criminal Offences Act, as well as the Law Reform Marriage and Divorce Act, applicable to non-Muslims, define marriage as that between a man and woman.

one built on equality. Cunie also described his relationship with his partner of more than ten years as one that was equal. Mitch and Cunie described what an equal relationship means to them and said that they did not think they were superior to their partners. Neither did they feel entitled to their partners or family life, and chores and family responsibilities were divided between them equitably.

Before delving into the gender relations related to equality as described by Cunie and Mitch, it is important to note two levels of social inequality that Mitch's family arrangement raises. While he referred to his partner as his "wife," they were not married. First, as discussed above, Mitch and his wife cannot be legally married as Malaysian law does not recognise same-sex marriage. In 2017, the court of appeal set aside the federal court's decision allowing a trans man to change his gender marker on his identity documents, citing a requirement for him to prove that he is biologically male, i.e. has XY chromosomes (Jalil, 5 January 2017). Second, both the Shariah laws and the civil law prohibit marriage between a Muslim and a non-Muslim, thus requiring a non-Muslim to convert in order to marry a Muslim. Upon divorce, the converting spouse is unable to convert out of Islam as this is considered apostasy and is unlawful under Shariah. Maznah Mohamad (2010, p. 368) states that it is never a clear-cut divide that the Shariah only governs Muslims while the civil judiciary is religion-blind or neutral when it comes to adjudications involving Muslim and non-Muslim litigants. The collusion of civil-Shariah governance had occurred with the emergence of new laws and regulations to support the Islamisation project. Matters pertaining to Islam and Muslims, therefore, do have consequences on members of the population who do not profess the religion. The Malaysian State is closely tied to Malay and Muslim identities. According to Maznah Mohamad (2010), this factor favours the state's Islamisation project, as well as marking the Malay/Muslim identity as the ascendant or superior one in Malaysia.

Race and the Hegemony of Masculinity in Malaysia

Mitch and Cunie's experiences of equality in their respective relationships may be contradictory to the model of Malay masculinity in Malaysia. Malay culture distinguishes between passion (*nafsu*) and reason (*akal*), where women are assumed to have more passion than reason (Peletz, 1995, p. 150). This view then led to women's role in public life—especially where decision-making is concerned—to be restricted, as reason is seen as superior to passion. However, gender roles are not so divided that it establishes men as

CHALLENGING MASCULINITY

the heads of households. Key scholars (Mohamad, 2010; Ong, 1995; Peletz, 1995) argue that the Malay culture has historically been gender-neutral, if not less patriarchal than what it is at present. The prevalent argument is that the changes that have led to a more patriarchal and detrimental division of gender and power stem from state projects to Islamise the governance of the country. The ideal Malaysian Malay-Muslim person is imagined as male, heteropatriarchal, and heterosexual, who must portray his dominance in the political, matrimonial, and family arenas, and demonstrate piety and ethics in accordance with institutional Islam (Goh, 2014, p. 606).

Hence, a Malay Muslim man is the head of the household and has the power and privilege that comes with that position. According to Maznah Mohamad (2010, p. 377), this gives rise to a new Malay-Muslim masculinity marked by male virility, multiple children borne by his wives, and active in the propagation of his faith, instead of focusing on duty and responsibility in the family. Shariah laws discriminate against women in matters of the family or division of property, inheritance, or matrimony such that reforms of the Shariah laws have changed Muslim family relations from being more bilateral to being more male-centred. Article 8 of the Malaysian Federal Constitution recognises that gender is not a basis for discrimination. However, real-life inequalities between the genders persist, as demonstrated through the subtle preferential treatment of men over women in political, religious, and socio-cultural areas, often culminating in the subordination of women (Goh, 2014, p. 606). In 2012, in the absence of the government's report, Malaysian women's rights NGOs submitted an alternative report to the Committee on the Elimination of all Forms of Discrimination against Women (WAO, 2012). The report highlights:

the continued under-representation of women in politics and decision-making positions and the lack of success of plans attempting to address this; the consistently low women's labour force participation rate; the lack of labour rights afforded to migrant domestic workers and their continued vulnerability to abuse; the non-recognition of refugees' identity; the legal permissibility of child marriage; the policing of morality; the lack of comprehensive, rights-based sex education; the difficulty women face in accessing their reproductive right to decide to have a child and to access high-quality health services; and the continued non-recognition of marital rape (WAO, 2012, p. 10).

The status of women in Malaysia remains far from equal. Male superiority over women in Malay-Muslim culture is further codified in the Shariah family law enactments across the different states in Malaysia. As Shariah law comes under the purview of the state administration, each state in Malaysia has its own version of family law enactments (Sisters in Islam, 2003). Sisters in Islam advocate for the reform of these Shariah laws towards enactments that are built on the principles of equality and justice, but these efforts are opposed by state actors through various religious bodies. In 2014, the Selangor Religious Council (MUIS) issued a fatwa,[8] which was gazetted by the government of the state of Selangor, declaring Sisters in Islam a deviant organisation subscribing to religious liberalism and pluralism (Yatim, 2019). The organisation is continuing its legal challenge of the fatwa. Perceptions of Malay and Muslim masculinity in terms of its superiority to femininity and its entitlements are not just socially and politically but also legally sanctioned by the state.

While the state may not be able to influence the decisions Mitch and Cunie made regarding equality in their relationships with their partners, it does have an influence on their decision-making in becoming men. Mitch and Cunie both decided that they would transition with their partners; they did not want to make any decisions on transitioning without the full support of their partners. Mitch's partner was at first apprehensive about him starting medical transitioning due to concerns over side effects and other medical-related matters. She and Mitch decided that they would gather as much information as possible to ensure a safe transitioning process before he began. She became fully supportive of him being on testosterone hormones. Cunie, however, had not been able to garner his partner's support, as her concerns were about transgender people not being accepted in Islam.

Aside from its impact on personal life, the Malay-Muslim identity also impacts trans men's social interactions with other Malaysians. Malaysia's political and economic history, preceding its colonial past, has imposed a deep division among the different ethnic communities. A contributing factor is also the privileged position of the Bumiputera[9] people (Malay and Indigenous communities), which is enshrined in the federal constitution. This entitles Bumiputera people to affirmative action policies and other economic policies garnered to increase their political and economic standing. These policies led to economic improvements amongst the Malays, but they were perceived to be at the cost of economic prosperity for other races, thus leading to resentment (Gomez & Jomo, 1999, p. 39). This resentment

---

8   Religious edict.
9   Malay for "sons of the soil." The category applies to Malays and Indigenous communities in Malaysia. The Bumiputera status does not automatically imply Muslim identity.

CHALLENGING MASCULINITY

is felt at the everyday level through social interactions. For example, Mitch recalled a verbal altercation he experienced when a Malay man verbally abused him after assuming he was Chinese. Mitch said that the Malay man's faulty assumption was evident in the way he spoke to Mitch—rude and crass. There is a longstanding animosity between the Malay and Chinese populations in Malaysia stemming from colonial policies of racial division of labour (Gabriel, 2015, p. 789). The British cultivated and perpetuated the stereotype of the "lazy native" as opposed to the hardworking Chinese and Indian migrants, intensifying antagonisms and entrenching differences between social groups. This antagonism continues in Malaysians' social and political lives as the superior position of Malays (*Ketuanan Melayu*)[10] is seen to be challenged especially by the Chinese (Husin Ali, 2008, p. xvii).

A more obvious example of this ethnic group resentment is seen in Hans's (Malay and Muslim) experience playing recreational futsal in a mixed-sex group:

> All of the Malay guys would sit on one side and they would be discussing among themselves and then there's this other side where the girls will be sitting and I think I would say that the other side is the minority because [the] Chinese and Indian [guys sit there too]. I think they also don't feel comfortable being in the Malay group.

Hans was uncomfortable around the Malay men in the group because they were loud—"they shout and curse a lot." They also spoke in a way that assumed familiarity, e.g. using words like *engkau* which is an informal word meaning "you" and is considered *kasar*.[11] Hans also noted what Liw had picked up on—that Malay men would shake each other's hands. It made Hans uneasy as he said he did "not like to be touched." The Malay men also referred to each other with words like *babi*,[12] which is often used derogatorily and has a racial connotation as it is commonly used to refer to Chinese people in Malaysia. Hans made a conscious decision to sit away from the Malay men, sitting instead with the women. Here, he noticed that the men from the racial minority groups—Chinese and Indian—also sat with the women. Hans said he was chastised by the Malay men for sitting with the women—something that the Chinese and Indian men escaped. The expectation of Hans to sit away from the women resonates

10 Malay for Malay supremacy.
11 Malay for rough or uncouth.
12 Malay for pig.

with earlier discussions of masculinity being defined as separation from femininity. That the Chinese and Indian men were not expected to do that raises the question of whether the Malay men recognised them as men at all. It is also possible that they did not see the need to police the Chinese and Indian men as they were only concerned about the behaviours of Malay men so as to maintain the politically ascribed superior position of the Malay race.

Hans's experience at the futsal court exemplifies the nuances of racialised everyday experiences in Malaysian life. I will use this to problematise Connell's (2005) concept of "hegemonic masculinity." The concept resonates with the Malaysian experience of masculinity in its positioning of women as subordinate to men. As exemplified by Malaysian women's rights NGOs in their report to CEDAW cited above, men dominate women in the private and public spheres in Malaysia. The hierarchies of masculinity are especially evident when inflected through race relations in Malaysia. There are parallels between Malay masculinity and Connell's (2005) hegemonic masculinity. As demonstrated by Maznah Mohamad (2010), considerable state resources have been invested in creating a hegemony of Malay Muslim masculinity. Hegemonic masculinity is defined as "the configuration of gender practice which embodies the currently accepted answer to the problem of the legitimacy of patriarchy, which guarantees (or is taken to guarantee) the dominant position of men and the subordination of women" (Connell, 1995, p. 77). Malay masculinity, in its present form, is seemingly consonant with Connell's argument that "hegemony is likely to be established only if there is some correspondence between cultural ideal and institutional power, collective if not individual" (Connell, 1995, p. 77).

The reforms to Shariah laws in Malaysia lend to the identity making of the Malay man that is focused on maleness, but exempt from the gender roles that are typically identified with it. The exalted Malay Muslim male is positioned as having more power over women and also men of other races. The tensions between the Malays and Chinese in Malaysia also exemplify the position that is conferred to the latter group. Practices such as polygamy, for example, which is prohibited for non-Muslim men, serve to define an identity for a group and "is the marker of a group homogenisation providing an excuse for distinctiveness and obviousness" (Mohamad, 2010, p. 377). These laws also strengthen the notion of Malay Muslim men's domination over women as symbolic of their power in society; the ideal Malay Muslim man is symbolised, per Maznah Mohamad (2010), by male virility and his wives bearing him many children, and establishes his position over the subordinate woman.

CHALLENGING MASCULINITY 137

However, there are ways in which the racialised gender relations in Malaysia diverge from Connell's (2005) concept of hegemonic masculinity. The definition of this concept requires all other men to position themselves in relation to it, thus using this as an ideal of masculinity to aspire to. Yet the narratives of Malaysian trans men show that they do not aspire to this idea of masculinity. Mitch and Hans protested this idea, even as Malay Muslim men. Damon (Indian) and Liw and Ben (Chinese) spoke about being grateful that they were not Muslim men. They thought it would infringe on their rights due to the various restrictions faced by Muslims in Malaysia. These restrictions have resulted in Malaysia ranking sixth out of 198 countries worldwide in terms of the degree of restrictions on freedom of religion (Moustaffa, 2018, p. 31). Backus (2017) considers Indian men as constituting the position of subordinated masculinity in Malaysia, and yet the Indian trans men (Damon, LaudeB, John, and Dorian) considered themselves as having more agency and power over their lives compared to Muslim men.

Scholars (Connell, 1998, p. 7; Ford & Lyons, 2012, p. 10; Wieringa et al., 2007, p. 4) call for consideration of globalisation and the world order in understanding gender relations. Hence, masculinities in Malaysia must be positioned against global ideas of power and masculinity. This, therefore, raises the question of global race relations and their intersections with gender. Firstly, there is the contention that the ideal of masculinity is white masculinity. This is exemplified by Connell's (2005) positioning of Black and other non-white masculinities as marginalised masculinity. Next is the role played by colonialism and imperialism in setting up the global order of politics and identities. Imperialism played a crucial role in creating gender divisions of labour, and gender ideologies were linked with racial hierarchies. The European gender order linking masculinity with the public and femininity with the private is an example of how Western ideas of labour division displaced many Indigenous practices (Connell, 2005, p. 8). The West is still very much perceived as white (Mohanty, 1988; Hall, 1990; Backus, 2017), and the masculine is always assumed to be white and heterosexual. Hence, that which is not masculine belongs to identities that are not white and heterosexual. The Western and white male is the ideal and, therefore, has the power to dictate the hegemony upon which hegemonic masculinity is constructed.

Race and religion do not only govern the interviewees' personal lives but also their social and political realities. I demonstrated how the state's role in governing race affects the construction of Malaysian men and their masculinities. The discussion in this section is but a snapshot of the complexities around race and gender relations in Malaysia. Nonetheless, trans men demonstrated their resistance to and challenge of dominant ideas of masculinity. Gender relations in the country remain strongly patriarchal, where one pathway is the state establishing patriarchal gender relations within the construction of an ideal of Malay Muslim masculinity.

Trans men navigate male privilege due to their outsider-within status, allowing them to perceive masculinity through their pre-transition experiences, where they were perceived and treated as women. This leads them to recognise and thus question the unearned biases they receive because they are now men. They make space for women in their workplace and speak up against sexual harassment. They also question gender stereotypes that assume women's lower status in relationships, leading them to suffer negative consequences in terms of social punishment from men and women. They recognise and apply their agency in deciding the kind of men they want to be and fashion their masculinity accordingly. In exercising their agency to question and challenge male privilege and dominant ideas of masculinity, trans men are exercising a different kind of privilege. In chapter 7, I build on this to demonstrate how interviewees proceed to develop their male identities separate from masculinity.

References

Abraham, C. (2004). *The naked social order.* Pelanduk Publications.

Asia Pacific Transgender Network (APTN). (2017). *Legal gender recognition in Malaysia: A legal and policy review in the context of human rights.* APTN.

Backus, R. (2017). *The double colonisation: Subjugated bodies and queer sexualities of Malaysian Indian men.* Lambert Academic Publishing.

Bandura, A. (2001). Social cognitive theory: An agentic perspective. *Annual Review of Psychology, 52*(1), 1–26. https://doi.org/10.1146/annurev.psych.52.1.1

Bernama. (20 March 2019). Kelantan to remain without cinemas. *The Sun Daily.* https://www.thesundaily.my/local/kelantan-to-remain-without-cinemas-FN708160

Bernama. (3 April 2020). Missing three Friday prayers during MCO does not make one a munafiq. https://www.astroawani.com/berita-malaysia/missing-three-friday-prayers-during-mco-does-not-make-one-munafiq-minister-236680

Case, K. A., Iuzzini, J., & Hopkins, M. (2012). Systems of privilege: Intersections, awareness and applications. *Journal of Social Issues, 68*(1), 1–10. https://doi.org/10.1111/j.1540-4560.2011.01732.x

Case, K. A., Hensley, R., and Anderson, A. (2014). Reflecting on Heterosexual and Male Privilege: Interventions to raise awareness. *Journal of Social Issues, 70*(4), 722 – 740. 10.1111/josi.12088

Collins, P. H. (1986). Learning from the outsider within: The sociological significance of Black feminist thought. *Social Problems, 33*(6), S14–S32. https://doi.org/10.1525/sp.1986.33.6.03a00020

Connell, R. (2005). *Masculinities* (2nd edition). Polity Press.

Eng, K. K. (2018). *Social cultural engineering and the Singaporean state*. Springer.

Ford, M., & Lyons, L. (2011). Introduction. In M. Ford & L. Lyons (Eds.), *Men and Masculinities in Southeast Asia* (pp. 1–19). Routledge.

Gabriel, P. S. (2015). The meaning of race in Malaysia: Colonial, post-colonial and possible new conjunctures. *Ethnicities, 15*(6), 782–809. https://doi.org/10.1177/1468796815570347

Goh, J. N. (2014). Fracturing interwoven heteronormativities in Malaysian Malay-Muslim masculinity: A research note. *Sexualities, 17*(5–6), 600–617. https://doi.org/10.1177/1363460714526317

Gomez, E. T., & Jomo, K. S. (1999). *Malaysia's political economy: Politics, patronage and profits*. Cambridge University Press.

Government of Malaysia. (1957) *Federal Constitution*. https://www.jac.gov.my/spk/images/stories/10_akta/perlembagaan_persekutuan/federal_constitution.pdf

Government of Malaysia. (1976) *Act 574 Penal Code*. https://ccid.rmp.gov.my/Laws/Act_574_Panel_Code_Malaysia.pdf

Hall, S. (1990). Cultural identity and diaspora. In P. Williams & L. Chrisman (Eds.), *Colonial discourse and post-colonial theory: A reader* (p. 392–403). Columbia University Press.

Husin Ali, S. (2008). *Ethnic relations in Malaysia: Harmony and conflict*. SIRD.

Jalil, M. A. (2017, 5 January). NRD wins appeal bid to stop transgender from changing IC details. *Malay Mail*. https://www.malaymail.com/news/malaysia/2017/01/05/nrd-wins-appeal-bid-to-stop-transgender-from-changing-ic-details/1286225

Jankowiak, W., & Xuan, L. (2014). The decline of the chauvinistic model of Chinese masculinity: A research report. *Chinese Sociological Review, 46*(4), 3–18. https://doi.org/10.2753/CSA2162-0555460401

Li, M., & Luo, Z. (2020). The 'bad women drivers myth': The overrepresentation of female drivers and gender bias in China's media. *Information, Communication & Society, 23*(5), 776–793. https://doi.org/10.1080/1369118X.2020.1713843

Mahaveera, S., & Hamdan, N. (2017, June 25). Malaysian female imam hits back at critics. *The Malaysian Insight*. https://www.themalaysianinsight.com/s/5973

Mandal, S. (2004). Transethnic solidarities, racialisation, and social equality. In E. T. Gomez (Ed.), *The state of Malaysia: Ethnicity, equity and reform* (pp. 49–78). Routledge Curzon.

Mohamad, M. (2010). Making majority, undoing family: Law, religion and the Islamisation of the state in Malaysia. *Economy & Society, 39*(3), 360–384. https://doi.org/10.1080/03085147.2010.486218

Mohanty, C. T. (1988). Under Western eyes: Feminist scholarship and colonial discourse. *Feminist Review, 30*(1), 61–88. https://doi.org/10.1057/fr.1988.42

Moustaffa, T. (2018). *Constituting religion: Islam, liberal rights and the Malaysian state.* Cambridge University Press.

Musa, M. F. (29 January 2024). "Mohd. Na'im Mokhtar: Business as usual in JAKIM?" *ISEAS Perspective.* https://www.iseas.edu.sg/articles-commentaries/iseas-perspective/2024-7-mohd-naim-mokhtar-business-as-usual-in-jakim-by-mohd-faizal-musa/

Ong, A. (1995). State versus Islam: Malay families, women's bodies and the body politic in Malaysia. In A. Ong & M. G. Peletz (Eds.), *Bewitching women, pious men: Gender and body politics in Asia* (pp. 159–194). University of California Press.

Pease, B. (2016). Critical social work with men: Challenging men's complicity in the reproduction of patriarchy and male privilege. *Social Alternatives, 35*(4), 49–53.

Peletz, M. G. (1995). Neither reasonable nor responsible: Contrasting representations of masculinity in Malay society. In A. Ong & M. G. Peletz (Eds.), *Bewitching women, pious men: Gender and body politics in Southeast Asia* (pp. 159–194). University of California Press.

Peretz, T. (2020). Seeing the invisible knapsack: Feminist men's strategic responses to the continuation of male privilege in feminist spaces. *Men and Masculinities, 23*(3–4), 447–475. https://doi.org/10.1177/1097184X18784990

Rao, R. (2020). *Out of time: The queer politics of postcoloniality.* Oxford University Press.

Schilt, K. (2006). Just one of the guys?: How transmen make gender visible at work. *Gender & Society, 20*(4), 465–490. https://doi.org/10.1177/0891243206288077

Shah, S. (2018). *The making of a gay Muslim: Religion, sexuality and identity in Malaysia and Britain.* Palgrave Macmillan.

Sisters in Islam (SIS). (2003). *Memorandum: Violation of Muslim women's human rights.* Sisters in Islam. https://sistersinislam.org/violation-of-muslim-womens-human-rights-further-discrimination-against-muslim-women-under-the-selangor-islamic-family-law-bill-2003-through-selective-gender-neutral-provisions/

Tee, K. (6 November 2020) In budget 2021, Putrajaya allocates RM1.4b for Islamic affairs under PM's dept. *The Malay Mail.* https://www.malaymail.com/news/malaysia/2020/11/06/in-budget-2021-putrajaya-allocates-rm1.4b-for-islamic-affairs-under-pms-dep/1920013

Towns, A. J., & Terry, G. (2014). "You're in that realm of unpredictability": Mateship, loyalty and men challenging men who use domestic violence against women. *Violence Against Women, 20*(8), 1012–1036. https://doi.org/10.1177/1077801214546232

Wieringa, S. E., Blackwood, E., & Bhaiya, A. (2007). Introduction. In S. E. Wieringa, E. Blackwood, & A. Bhaiya (Eds.) *Women's sexualities and masculinities in a globalising Asia* (p. 4). Palgrave Macmillan.

Women's Aid Organisation (WAO). (2012). *The status of women's human rights: 24 years of CEDAW in Malaysia.* WAO. https://wao.org.my/wp-content/uploads/2019/01/The-Status-of-Womens-Human-Rights-24-Years-of-CEDAW-in-Malaysia.pdf

Yatim, H. (27 August 2019). Selangor fatwa declaring Sisters in Islam a deviant group stands—high court. https://theedgemalaysia.com/article/selangor-fatwa-declaring-sisters-islam-deviant-group-stands-%E2%80%94-high-court https://www.theedgemarkets.com/article/selangor-fatwa-declaring-sisters-islam-deviant-group-stands-%E2%80%94-high-court

Yuen, M. (11 October 2019). Budget 2020: JAKIM welcomes increase in allocations for Islamic affairs. *The Star Daily.* https://www.thestar.com.my/news/nation/2019/10/11/budget-2020-jakim-welcomes-increase-in-allocations-for-islamic-affairs

7.   Rejecting Masculinity?

Abstract: Using a qualitative approach, 23 in-depth semi-structured interviews were analysed to gain a perspective on trans men's decision-making about their masculine identities. This chapter interrogates the decision-making that interviewees embark on upon reconciling their female histories with their male identities and lives as men. Utilising concepts of agency and self-determination, the chapter demonstrates how interviewees challenge prevalent ideas of masculinity and explore new ways of embodying manhood and masculinities that are reflective of their own values and beliefs and not societal expectations.

Keywords: trans men, Malaysia, decision-making, agency, self-determination

Trans people in Malaysia embody a dual existence, where they are male and female at the same time because gender markers on their identity documents cannot be changed. They carry this duality with them in every moment of their daily lives. Their present and future selves will, until legal gender recognition becomes available, always be held ransom by their past selves who are a different gender from them. For trans men, acknowledging a "female" identity and history can be contentious as it raises the question of whether they were female at all. The term FTM (female to male) is sometimes used to acknowledge, as Jason Cromwell (1999, p. 28) calls it, their "female socialisation and history." Others may prefer the term "trans man" to mark their distance from anything that connotes female or feminine. Both terms, however, are interchangeable. Even though trans men may never have identified as female, or had experience of being socialised as such, there is always, at some physical level, an awareness of having a history as female, if for no other reason than being assigned such at birth (Cromwell, 1999, p. 29).

Trans men are required to reconcile this aspect of their identities and bodies, resulting in them disrupting ideas of masculinity and also heterosexuality. By doing this, they raise a contradiction in their existence and

---

Kumaresan, Vizla. *Trans Men in Malaysia: Decision-Making, Masculinity and Manhood.* Amsterdam: Amsterdam University Press, 2025.
DOI: 10.5117/9789048562596_CH07

have to negotiate their gender to find a balance between the masculine and feminine. This contradiction is a crucial element in the process of decision-making as it allows trans men to reconcile their masculine identities based on their values and judgements and not on heuristics or stereotypes of masculinity. Their female histories allow trans men to recognise unearned biases in their interactions with people. They come to experience the limits of masculinity, especially with regard to the human experience of emotions and how expectations of masculinity restrict their abilities to feel or express those emotions.

Trans men's female histories pose a challenge to their personal identities but also place them in a position to question masculinity's prerogative to subjugate femininity. They challenge the central idea of the hegemony of masculinity, which is men's dominance over women. This challenges the binaric model of gender by de-linking masculinity from men. Masculinity is not a property of individuals; like femininity, it is part of doing gender (West & Zimmerman, 1987, p. 126). Hence, men, as well as women, can be masculine by moving through and producing masculinity by engaging in masculine practices. By distancing themselves from traditional ideas of masculinity, trans men do not make masculinity redundant in their identities but displace its centrality in the decisions they make about themselves in becoming men. I will demonstrate in the sections below that they make these decisions based on their own values and beliefs.

Embracing the Feminine

The concept of masculinity is constructed as predominantly dependent on a binary model, where it exists always in contrast with femininity. For masculinity to exist, be identified, and be reproduced, it must be opposite to and separate from femininity. Recognising this becomes a source of questioning for the trans men; as Blue stated: "I don't want [to be] a man [if it] makes me lose traits of my femininity. So sometimes when people [refer to me as] man, I feel that way. Does me being a man mean leaving my feminine side?" Having arrived at a point in his transitioning where he was confident in identifying as a man, Blue recognised that he had feminine traits which he identified as being an essential part of who he is as a person. His conflict was in managing expectations of denying these feminine traits to fit into society's perceptions of masculinity. He continued, "I would feel uncomfortable when [men] behave in a very manly way. This is me. Is me being not [as] manly enough to be a manly gesture?" Blue's recognition that

REJECTING MASCULINITY?   145

he was not masculine in the way other men were did not lead him to doubt
his masculinity. Not feeling pressured to change his ways to fit into the
masculine ideal, he hoped that his masculinity was perceived as "enough."
Damon, too, felt the same about his masculinity:

> So if I am going to be a man I have to do [my] way a bit even though it's
> slightly feminine. That's what [men] think. It's fine. I feel like I am very
> much more attractive to women because I am not just being an ass.

Damon acknowledged that he had elements of femininity and did not
see any incentive to change his mannerisms to be more stereotypically
masculine. Damon and Blue negotiated the privileges that came from com-
plying with the hegemonic ideals of masculinity when they embraced what
they referred to as their feminine sides. However, there were some perks
that came with their portrayal of masculinity. Damon recognised that he
received a lot of attention from women; he said, "women find me more
attractive than cis guys." This is part of the pedestal effect observed amongst
men who identify as feminist, which complicates the work of challenging
hegemonic masculinity and practices, as changing individual practices of
men highlights the continued implication of the structure of patriarchy in
changing gender relations. Nonetheless, men's responses to such unearned
privileges—rejecting them, for instance—plays an important role in the
continued and necessary challenge of the patriarchal constructs governing
gender relations. In Damon's case, this is highlighted in the way he managed
the extra attention that came his way. He was deliberate in his intentions
to be respectful of the women who expressed romantic or sexual interest in
him and maintained that he would remain monogamous in his relationship
with his girlfriend. Here, Damon was refusing the complicity that comes
with abiding by the ideals of hegemonic masculinity.

Notably, Damon learnt much about masculinity from his father, whose
abusive behaviours informed him of the kind of man he did not want to
be. He also firmly believed in gender equality and challenged cisgender
men's expectations of him to be more dominant in his relationship with his
girlfriend. Damon had come to deem these kinds of behaviours "behaving
like an ass," which have been reinforced by the men he has come to know
since transitioning. He found the behaviours that these men displayed
to be physically and sexually aggressive. He told me about a party he
attended with his girlfriend's colleagues. Her manager, a cisgender man,
became physically aggressive with Damon in an attempt to gain his
girlfriend's attention. At another casual gathering, this same manager

was friendly with Damon and spoke to him about using his good looks to gain multiple female sexual partners. These were the exact kinds of homosocial behaviours that Damon despised and was repulsed by. Studies (McMillan & Paul, 2011) have demonstrated that when men have to defend their mothers from their abusive fathers, they develop motivation for redefining their own masculinities. Damon's experience of violence, along with having to defend his mother from his father, played a significant role in his decision-making on masculinity. For this, he knew he would experience (or anticipate) social sanctions for not being stereotypically masculine. Damon, like Blue, did not engage in acts of aggression and did not subscribe to a hypersexual idea of sexuality or see women as sexual conquests. These aspects mark them as "feminine" in the eyes of men and some women.

Embracing Emotionality

Trans men discover that they must also come to terms with their emotionality. Squaring up with the expectation of stoicism, they came to recognise an emptiness when they were unable to express emotions—especially sadness. Blue experienced an inhibition in his ability to cry during his first few months on hormones. He felt "heavy," and this feeling was only relieved when he could finally cry and experience the release. Mitch, too, talked about being unable to cry and watching a tear-jerking Hindi film multiple times to force a release and weep. White Lotus also spoke about emotions in relation to femininity, where his mother and sister did not see him as a man because he was "emotional":

> Their idea of what a man is [is] way too messed up. Like when you're a man you can't cry. Or, [if] you're a man why do you feel that way. Because you're not supposed to feel. I think that is ridiculous. It's come to a point where my brother doesn't understand what crying is all about. Why is that? He's a child. He shouldn't stop crying. He should cry when he wants to cry.

From his mother and sister, White Lotus experienced a common stereotypical expectation of masculinity as being stoic. It is the idea that emotions are in the domain of that which is woman. Stoicism in men has been found to be linked to interpersonal difficulties and correlates with men's lower state of well-being, leading researchers to believe that stoicism is a potentially maladaptive coping mechanism (Murray et al., 2008, p. 1379). The trans men

I spoke to for this study struggle with this expectation as they were raised as female and were not subjected to the expectation that "boys don't cry."

Jake was the only trans man who reported hearing the refrain "boys don't cry; they bleed" from the father of another boy at a playground. Though it was not an idea prevalent in his family, Jake tried to practice it. However, despite his best efforts he could not bring himself to stop crying during periods of sadness. After an initial phase of doubting his own masculinity, Jake arrived at a point of reconsidering the phrase and questioning its relevance. Trans men, like Jake, carry within their bodies their histories of having lived life as female (even though they may reject the identity) and therefore carry with them the habits and practices from this time—emotions in this instance. Their bodies were inevitably marked as female—not just the physical aspects, but also histories of experiences. When speaking about histories or remnants of femininity, Miles, too, spoke about emotions:

> I don't think it's good to be on one side of things. It's not a binary. I think it's mainly trying to be empathetic as much as possible. And in terms of emotions I think that's very important. The whole men shouldn't speak so much. Keep [it] inside. I don't think that works because I've seen it in my family [and] how it doesn't help the family. My dad being all I don't talk about my feelings; I don't even tell my wife I love her things like that have really affected the family. I learned from seeing that, like what not to do. And then seeing how my mom and dad relate to each other.

Rejecting a binaric view of gender as either masculine or feminine, Miles saw the value of choosing to see emotionality as a human aspect. This allowed him to interpret emotionality as being empathetic. Like Damon, Miles had learnt from his father the elements of stereotypical masculinity that can be damaging. He attributed the breakdown of his parents' marriage to his father refusing to connect emotionally with others. Miles had come to value the importance of emotional connection for building relationships with others, especially his partner. Dines reported the same experience with his current partner.

Empathy plays a crucial role in building kinship and strong relationships involving men; it results in men experiencing more fulfilling relationships devoid of violence (McMillan & Paul, 2011). This differs from men using their feelings to manufacture a crisis to claim victimhood at the hands of women and feminism (Allan, 2016). In manufacturing crises, men's feelings are used as exhortations against women supposedly encroaching on what is thought of as male arenas in society and work. The trans men here, on the other hand, spoke of emotions because they wanted to feel what they felt in order to connect with their own sense of self as well as others, as this communicated to them information about themselves and others.

Embracing Femininity, Challenging Masculinity

While growing in comfort with their own masculinity, the trans men came to learn that women felt differently about it. While Miles, Dines, and Damon experienced external validation from acknowledging the feminine in them through emotional connections with their partners, they faced ambivalent responses from some women. Miles spoke about what it was like dating women before he met his current partner:

> It's just the element of femininity. Sure girls [say they] like guys who are in touch with their emotions and that part of feminine side. But when it comes to other kinds of feminine expression [it's] not really something they like. But I feel, in general, I'm not ideal boyfriend material for a lot of women in Malaysia who like men.

Alexis, too, had found that women did not find him attractive. In stepping away from ideals of hegemonic masculinity and embracing their feminine histories in the construction of their masculine identities, a factor that trans men came to contend with is the expectations of heterosexuality that are placed on them. The binaric gender construct expects masculinity and femininity to be complementary to, while being distant from, each other. Trans men had a taste of this expectation pre-transition, where expectations of heterosexuality were used to discipline them into femininity. When transitioning, it was used, instead, to discipline them into a stereotyped idea of heterosexual masculinity.

A successful portrayal of masculinity must be that which is romantically or sexually appealing to women—to get the girls, as exemplified by Damon's girlfriend's colleague. Challenging ideas of masculinity, then, necessitates challenging the idea of heterosexuality and that it is natural. The laws that govern what is natural supposedly dictate that men are active and dominant over women who are passive and submissive. Trans men, therefore, disrupt multiple ideas—manhood, masculinity, and heterosexuality—when they embrace the feminine within their portrayal of masculinity. The proximity of the feminine positions trans men in a subordinate position, as it does with gay men (Connell, 2005). Gay trans men like Jameel frequently get asked why they transitioned at all if they are going to be in relationships with men. Trans men's proclaiming of their male identities and manhood, therefore, also strengthens the notion that gender expression, gender identity, and sexuality are discrete and not mutually exclusive to each other.

Trans men also challenge the idea of what is natural or assumed to be essential in aspects of sex and gender, and that gender stems from sex. An example of this can be seen in Hans's experience of his girlfriend's sexual expectations of him:

> My girlfriend asked me why I never spank her [when we have sex]. I just told her that I don't like doing that. It's violent. Why would I want to be doing that? I love you. But she said isn't that what most men love doing? I think you know sometimes she thinks that I'm a bit too soft. But I honestly don't feel anything wrong with that. Sometimes I feel like my girlfriend is more masculine than me.

While Hans was comfortable with his expression of masculinity, he considered his girlfriend telling him he was "too soft." To heed her exhortations to "toughen up," he signed up to play futsal. She chastised him when he told her he had to learn to do things like fix electrical items or leaking pipes. She expected that he knew how to do these tasks simply because he was a man. For her, his expression of masculinity came naturally from his identity as a man. In expecting Hans to "spank her" when they had sex because "most men do," his girlfriend was expressing the belief that men are naturally violent and receive sexual gratification from sexual violence. Hans's girlfriend expected him to express violence for her benefit in terms of protecting her from other men:

> There was one time when she asked me if somebody came to me and wanted to *pukul*[1] me would [I] *pukul* him? And I told her that instead of prolonging the violence why don't we just stop and ask him why did you *pukul* her. And then she says but I want you to *pukul* him for me.

Hans's girlfriend was, firstly, expecting to face violence from a man, even in a hypothetical situation. Furthermore, she expected him to protect her from the hypothetical violence perpetrated by other men. The pacifist and non-violent solution of de-escalation was less appealing than violent retaliation. Again, she expected the binaric complementarity of gender and

1   Malay for hit or beat.

conflated men and violence. Hans's masculinity was assumed to be the natural opposite of her femininity. Here, Hans's masculinity is understood as being the (natural) role of protector to her feminine vulnerable/victim. Hans's girlfriend understood men as a set of stereotypes and utilised masculinity as a heuristic. Her use of heuristics demonstrates that it is a tool used not only by men to organise their behaviours but also by women to understand and organise gender relations with men. Femininity also becomes a set of heuristics. These heuristics become relatively simple guidelines for behaviour that take the place of more careful, effortful, and therefore complex analyses that humans are generally reluctant to undertake due to cognitive miserliness (O'Neil et al., 2017).

Hans's girlfriend learnt these heuristics about masculinity because that was how the male gender had been constructed for her; her expectations of Hans were based on how her father was. Accordingly, Damon had constructed heuristics about masculinity that, for him, corresponded with "being an ass." These heuristics gain strength based on frequency of use. Furthermore, the idea that men are violent is a prevalent one. All the trans men in this study had experiences with GBV, where the perpetrators were men. The connection between men and violence was, therefore, true for the trans men as well as the women in their lives. However, many argue that violence is far more complex than that which is situated within the bodies of men. Since feminist analysis can blame individual men for women's oppression, men's power has come to be situated as something primordial instead of lying in the social arrangements, systems, and structures that institutionalise men's power (Segal, 2001, p. 101).

Acknowledging that men are the main perpetrators of physical and sexual violence against women, activists such as Gary Barker (2016) caution against the use of the term male violence. Calling it patriarchal violence, instead, allows for the understanding of violence as based on complex power relations. This perspective will allow for a fuller analysis of not just GBV, but also men's violence against each other. Violence is caused by systemic factors—patriarchy and capitalism—that lead to social inequalities, which, when coupled with rigid ideas of masculinity, can lead to men committing violence. Patriarchal gender relations resulting in men's lack of social connection—displays of affection from their loved ones and relations with family and community—lead to them being more likely to commit acts of violence against others. Studying men from Central America who actively reject hegemonic notions of masculinity in their efforts to keep themselves and their families safe from the drug trade reveals that the men come to have their decision affirmed by the incentive of loving and close relationships with their partners and children (McMillan & Paul, 2011). Evidence, thus, indicates that violence perpetrated by men is not inevitable. Even when living in violent environments, men can make decisions not to act violently with others. Evidence points to the role played by factors like self-regulation when it comes to men exercising power and using violence in private life.

Embracing Femininity, Experiencing Agency

Popular culture, through shows like *Narcos* (2015–2017), has come to link Central America with the dangerous and violent international drug trade involving men knowingly perpetrating violence to favour profit and riches. Yet, there are men in the region who refuse to participate in the trade. Anita McMillan and Moli Paul (2011) demonstrate that these men reject ideas of masculinity espoused by the drug trade through the exercise of agency, where they can make different decisions for themselves. These men do not think that the conditions of their lives are inevitable, nor that they have no control over what happens to them or how they happen.

Trans men had already demonstrated agency in being reflexive in their observations about themselves as men in making decisions about masculinity. Instead of cognitive tools such as heuristics, they utilised standards that they set for their own behaviours, which they then responded to by evaluating their own actions and behaviours. Internal factors—feelings and thoughts—become tools for decision-making and subsequent actions. This self-regulation requires the interplay between self-observation and the ability to judge the impact of their actions, and then to attune their reactions to their behaviours and their consequent effects.

This model of behaviour, as Bandura (1986) suggests, relies on internal standards and evaluative methods in self-regulation. Internal standards "are developed from information conveyed by different modes of social influence," which include modelling, personal experiences, and validation (Bandura, 1986, p. 336). Trans men base their ideas of masculinity on models available in their families and social circles and then adapt them based on what they had experienced as females, and then while living as male and then having those behaviours validated (or not) by others. These processes have helped develop the internal standards that enable them to make decisions about their masculine identities. They reflect on and evaluate their own experiences in their decision-making process. They are keen and sensitive observers of others' reactions to them, as this is an important indicator of the validity of their performance of masculinity.

Trans men develop a repertoire of ways of being and doing feminine and masculine, and they make decisions to exhibit these or not based on the process suggested above. Thus, they can make decisions about becoming and being men, not based on gender but on the kind of people they want to be and how they think and feel. Their emotions, along with cognitive dissonance which also results in feelings of displeasure, play a role in their decision-making.

Trans men integrate their female histories into their sense of self as men, and, in so doing, they challenge the notion that masculinity must come with rejecting femininity. Although they face censure from cisgender men and women who judge them as not being man/ly enough, they remain resolute in their decision to embrace their feminine histories as it enables them to freely access and express their emotions, allowing them to build and have fulfilling relationships with others, especially their partners. Trans men's decisions to integrate the feminine into their identities force a re-thinking of the normalised connection between sex and gender. They challenge the assumption that gender stems from sex and that gender is a binary; for trans men, it can be anything they want it to be. Finally, trans men challenge heterosexuality by showing that the genders do not have to be complementary, raising challenges in their personal relationships as they bring forth heteronormative gender relations which assume binaric complementarity. In the following section, I will explore how, in integrating the feminine, trans men are able to negotiate their masculinity and engage complex thinking processes in decision-making about being men in ways that do not privilege these ideas of masculinity.

Imagining a New Manhood

Trans men challenge the idea of masculinity by embracing their feminine histories. By allowing themselves to integrate their feminine histories into their sense of self, the trans men disrupt the idea that the masculine is that which is not feminine. Doing this also disrupts heteronormative ideas of gender, whereby they challenge the binaric complementarity of masculinity and femininity. Since they encounter the limits of masculinity as a heuristic, they engage what Kahneman (2011) refers to as system 2 thinking in their decision-making about masculinity, allowing them to negotiate masculinity. I propose two factors that make it possible for trans men to engage in system 2 thinking: (1) a sense of agency and (2) the contradictions that they experience as trans men.

Kahneman (2011) explains that the systems theory of cognition proposes two decision-making systems. System 1 operates automatically and quickly, with little or no effort and no sense of voluntary control. System 2, on the other hand, allocates attention to the effortful mental activities that demand it, thus associating it with the subjective experience of agency, choice, and concentration. In Bandura's (2001, p. 2) conception of agency:

To be an agent is to intentionally make things happen by one's actions. Agency embodies endowments, belief systems, self-regulatory capabilities and distributed structures and functions through which personal influence exercised, rather than residing as a discrete entity in a particular place. The core features of agency enable people to play a part in their self-development, adaptation, and self renewal with changing times.

Trans men experience using their agency in their process of transitioning by taking an active role in their processes of becoming by learning and applying judgement on the aspects of masculinity they want to embody. The combined roles of agency and self-regulation in their decision-making around masculinity can be seen in this quote from Damon. He came to see men as "asses" because of what he learnt about masculinity from his father and the men in his family and social circles. His girlfriend's colleague reacted to him being nice:

You're so nice. You're so nice. I [told him] because I choose not to be an ass. That is why. Is [there] a problem [with] me being nice? My dad is an ass so I choose not to be an ass. I choose not to do things that are going to offend people.

Damon was adamant that he could make choices to ensure he never became the kind of man his father was. Through studying Central American men resisting hegemonic masculinity via the drug trade, McMillan and Paul identify that crucial to the study's participants being able to negotiate masculinity is their ability to think about their thoughts, consequently giving their thoughts and actions direction. The ability to shape the direction of actions also determined how Hans performed his masculinity. He said, "Well if I want to fit in into the normal masculine yeah [I can]. But it's so tiring." Hans's decision-making is based on the consequence he desired—in this case, more energy for himself.

Another key feature playing a role in decision-making about masculinity is relationships. Trans men demonstrate value for this in deciding not to commit violence in their lives or harm or offend others. This would require trans men to pay attention to other people's reactions—behaviours, speech, facial expressions—to determine if they are behaving appropriately or offensively. They must be able to understand the internal world of others and recognise when they have behaved or acted inappropriately. This requires them to be able to think about and feel the world from other people's perspective. This kind of social decentring is a skill that depends on social cognitive abilities such as person perception, attribution, decision-making, deduction, strategic planning, emotional intelligence, and general social information processing. It requires the ability to imagine one's self in another person's situation. This ability to represent the internal world of others triggers the effortful, slow, and reflective system 2 thinking because it causes people to believe in two contradictory responses simultaneously.

An example of this can be seen in Liw's preference to be seen as a man rather than masculine: "[I prefer] man because female[s] can also have the masculine side of them." Liw had come to understand that gender is socially constructed as binaric and complementary. His experience with his girlfriend forced him to reevaluate his stereotyped ideas of masculinity and femininity. She was an accomplished personal fitness trainer and they ran their business together. He had observed that she defied the typical expectations of femininity, therefore challenging his preconceived notions of masculinity as well. He felt disgusted when male gym goers insisted on working with male personal trainers or laughed at the abilities (or perceived lack of) female personal trainers. Miles also told me he did not view gender as a binary. For him, thinking beyond the construct of gender as a binary helped him reconcile his female history and accept that his ability to empathise and feel did not negate his masculinity.

Both Liw and Miles challenged the heuristics of masculinity they had come to learn from their environments. Stereotypes are a memory structure that, like heuristics, aid in decision-making (Prati et al, 2015, p. 802). Thinking of counterstereotypes encourages people to make a shift from a heuristic, categorical mode of impression formation to a more generative, individuated mode of impression formation. Engaging with counterstereotypes—information that conflicts with the stereotypes—leads people to utilise cognitive flexibility whereby they have to actively engage in adapting to new information and environments and apply creative thinking tools to find solutions to novel situations. The counterstereotypes lead to a shift from heuristics to a more systematic and analytical style of thinking. Experiencing masculinity and femininity in the ways that they have allows trans men to think beyond

REJECTING MASCULINITY?   155

stereotypes. They come to be less reliant on heuristics because they have experienced a conflict between these stereotypes and counterstereotypes.

For trans men, the contradictions also come from being man and not man at the same time. They experience this from living with identity documents that insist they are female and from standards set by hegemonic masculinity because their bodies are marked as female. Damon spoke of his experience with cisgender men:

> I do pass and when I meet my girlfriend's friends they have no idea. We were hanging out at the pool] and I just sat [outside the pool]. I thought, you know what? I am just going to [tell them I am trans]. And, the minute I [told] him he asked me [if I] have done any surgery yet. I said no. He treated me totally [differently] after that. I guess he started treating me like someone who has not transitioned. You haven't done your surgeries so you can't actually say you're a man.

The cisgender men that he befriended did not regard Damon as a man because he had undergone neither top nor bottom surgeries. He was, however, on testosterone hormone therapy. Connell's hierarchies of masculinities account for how social structures such as class and race create further relationships between masculinities, resulting in marginalisation. While the model does not specify transgender identity as grounds for marginalisation, I propose that it is, as the identity is in contestation with cis maleness that authorises power to the dominant group. This power relation between cis and trans men will exist while gender relations are seen as binaric and complementary. So, a man must have a penis (and lack ovaries and a uterus) in relation to a woman having a vagina (with ovaries and a uterus capable of pregnancy resulting in live childbirth). A trans man's lack of male genitals, therefore, means that he is not man enough. Added to this is the state of precarity that interviewees find themselves in, as experienced by Asher:

> When I first started [testosterone] I was very excited. Finally like a huge step of becoming myself. Like I know it's very cliche but it's like [I am getting] there and things like that. But honestly speaking as the process goes on, there is definitely that point where you feel like no matter how much you transition you can never get there. Like how cis guys are.

Asher's quote spoke to his experiences of never quite fitting in. His fluid gender expression meant that other people did not think he fit the socially approved masculine gender expression. He was constantly compared to cis men, whom he felt he may never be able to emulate. Ben expressed the same sentiment—that he "will never be like cis guys." This meant that Asher and Ben would always be scrutinised for their expression of masculinity (or not), thus making it difficult to pass as not trans (see chapter 4), leaving them in a precarious position with concerns for their safety. Their precarity is linked with gender norms where those whose performance of gender does not conform to social expectations are subjected to violence and harassment. Butler (2009, p. 2) argues that precarity "characterises that politically induced condition of maximised vulnerability and exposure for populations exposed to arbitrary state violence and to other forms of aggression that are not enacted by states and against which states do not offer adequate protection." The lack of legal gender recognition for transgender people in Malaysia means that the state is actively complicit in their vulnerability and the ensuing violence and harassment that they experience or come to expect.

Expectations to distance themselves from their bodies, and to even find them revolting, result in another form of conflict for trans men when they came to embrace their female histories. This conflict was felt deeply by White Lotus:

> I didn't [like being identified as female]. Being called a woman made me feel really out of place because when people call me a woman I [feel like] I should be proud of it [because] I have female genitalia and I grew up in a family where being a woman is something that you should be proud of. To me when you call me a woman I'd just be sitting there and thinking to myself like is that the right pronoun? When someone called me a boy I would immediately feel over the moon.

White Lotus had not begun medical transitioning. While he presented as male, he was sometimes perceived by others as female. His conflict arose from wanting to be referred to as male, coming at the cost of having to impugn his female history. He was raised to believe that being female did not make one inferior. Moreover, he attended a girl's school where he was inculcated with ideas of female empowerment. This kind of conflict leads to the cognitive strain that mobilises system 2 thinking. When system 2 is activated, a person is engaged—more alert, more intellectually active, less willing to be satisfied with superficially attractive answers, and more sceptical about their intuitions (Kahneman, 2011, p. 46). Engaging system 2 thinking means people are less likely to resort to automatic thoughts and ideas. It requires a person to deliberately seek information that they lack. The operations of system 2 are often associated with the subjective experience of agency, choice, and concentration. I have already proposed that the interviewees express and experience their own sense of agency in the active construction of their selves as men. By extension, they will be able to utilise this ability to make more deliberate decisions about masculinity.

However, conflict does not always result in the engagement of system 2 thinking. Cunie was able to rationalise his father's abusive behaviours towards his mother. Believing in gender equality, Cunie believed that men and women have their separate roles that are complementary. A good relationship, thus, relies on a compatibility between the roles played by the man and woman. He struggled in his relationship with his partner, who refused to accept that he was a man. His partner's refusal of his identity had a direct effect on Cunie's decisions regarding pursuing medical transitioning. However, he maintained that his reticence to medically transition was due to his own disagreement with transgender rights activists. He believed that it was not "right" for transgender people to claim political rights such as legal gender recognition. Doing so, he said, would bring unwanted attention to transgender people. He believed, instead, that transgender people should focus on working hard and making a good living to look after themselves. Cunie relied on stereotypes—gender roles being one—to give meaning to his life. He saw his role as provider—as husband and father—as his life's priority. The difficulties that he faced as a transgender person in Malaysia were dismissed because he believed his role to provide was more important. Cunie engaged in system justification, utilising social and psychological processes to legitimise existing social arrangements even if it came at the expense of personal and group interests.

Challenging Stereotypes

Many of the trans men saw the limits of gender stereotypes for themselves and others. It limited their options and pathways to being men. John was satisfied to know that he was a man and had little concern about masculinity. Although Damon expressed distress about the challenges that came with the absence of legal gender recognition in Malaysia, he was proud of his identity as a trans man. He did not feel threatened when cisgender men challenged his identity. Jervind said: "For me image is no longer important. Because there are some people [who] will accept [and] some people [who] will not. How I look [at] myself is more important. I am a man." For these trans men, their focus was not on performing masculinity but embodying their personhood. Being men, for them, was about living according to their values and ideals. Barker (2005) cites resistance as the ability that some men have to position themselves outside hegemonic or hyper masculinity. This resistance entails men challenging rigid or violent versions of manhood without giving up aspects of masculinity that they like, e.g. playing sports. Resistant masculinity, according to Barker (2005), does not mean rejecting masculinity. Instead, it calls for building a sense of masculinity around culturally relevant skills that allow them to feel secure in achieving a non-violent and more gender-equitable version of manhood. In that sense, trans men exhibit a resistant form of masculinity as they are able to anchor their identities to aspects of masculinity that they are comfortable with while thinking about and negotiating other aspects of masculinity based on what feels appropriate for them. For example, Liw felt the need to be able to financially support his partner while respecting her right to work and earn a living. While seeming contrary, his ability to do so confirms to him his sense of identity as a man. For him, it was important that his partner felt financially secure so that she could do what she desired in life. He wanted to provide a safety net for her. Liw differed from Cunie in that he did not depend on this gender role for his identity. Liw's partner did not expect him to fulfil this role; their relationship was not built on a notion of binaric complementarity of gender like Cunie's.

Gender relations play a role in the trans men feeling secure to move away from traditional ideas of masculinity. There is an important role played by heterosexual men's female partners, wives, or girlfriends in supporting the men's decisions to portray an alternative masculinity (Barker, 2005, p. 144). Liw, Mitch, Damon, Miles, and Dines experienced this in their relationship with their partners. Cunie's partner, however, expected him to play a more traditional masculine role in their relationship. White Lotus struggled with his decisions as his mother and sister expected a more traditional portrayal of masculinity. Aside from this, a supportive social environment—friends or other sources of social connection—also plays a role in affirming these decisions. Trans men demonstrate this by actively selecting their social circles. Alexis, John, and Ben moved away from men who displayed more hegemonic or hyper masculine traits. Mitch, Shane, Damon, Dorian, and Jameel drew support from other trans men with whom they had formed friendships and a sense of community. All of these actions affirm their sense of agency and also build a more affirming environment where they do not experience a need to express a masculinity that they are not comfortable with.

Imagining New Ways of Being Men

As much as these trans men had come to accept their masculine identities as projects that require their assertion of agency, they were still left with the conundrum of what to do with their female histories. Embracing it meant their masculine identities were scrutinised, as exemplified by Alexis's experience. Having fluid gender expression, Alexis enjoyed putting on makeup, dressing up, and wearing women's clothes. He learnt to apply makeup after he started medical transitioning. He was concerned that people would dismiss his male identity as well as the hours he spent practising putting on makeup if they discovered his female history. Speaking of his anticipation of people's responses to finding out he was assigned female at birth, he said: "Using pronouns. Just disrespect that I want to be treated as a man. Use my legal name. I got my name changed for a fucking reason." The proximity of the female to masculinity sparks an identity crisis, not only for the men themselves but also for others. John MacInnes (1998, p. 2) argues that gender does not exist and that masculinity is a trait that belongs to men and women. In this view, masculinity exists as an ideal or fantasy about what men should be like, and gender exists only as a result of a socialisation process that confirms men's power over women for the continuation of patriarchy. Any challenge of this order leads to a crisis in masculinity, and one of the sources of this crisis is women's increasing involvement in labour outside the home, with the ensuing quest for equality in society. Men have been shown to retaliate with violence when the quests for equality have been perceived as threats to (white) male privilege (MacInnes, 1998; Kimmel & Ferber, 2000; and Coston & Kimmel, 2012). However, experiences such as that of fisherman in Newfoundland have shown that applying appropriate problem-solving skills to deal with the changes in the industry that affect men's sense of manhood is less likely to result in a crisis of masculinity (Power, 2005). Cultivating a more resilient form of masculinity is an appropriate response to situations where traditional ideas of masculinity are challenged.

The trans men in this study did not see the proximity of the female in their masculine identities as a sign of crisis. Instead, they saw the feminine was something positive, even when it is disparaged by others. This insight arose from a sense of agency over the construction of not just their masculine identities but also their selves. This was evident to them when they recognised that they did not have to choose the kinds of masculine that were discordant with their values and beliefs. They could choose to not be an "ass," hence not repeat the violence they had witnessed and even experienced themselves. They could also negotiate the male privilege that they had come to experience as men by seeing and recognising privilege to address it. Again, it required the making of conscious decisions to challenge male privilege because they believed in gender equality; every one of the respondents in this study expressed abhorrence for any form of gender inequality and discussed ways in which they worked to build a more egalitarian relationship with the women in their lives.

In embracing their feminine histories and de-stabilising the definition of masculinity, and the notion of gender being binaric and complementary, trans men imagine new ways of being men. They become less reliant on stereotypes or heuristics of masculinity and deliberately think about how they want to be men because they experience contradictions in their experiences due to facing counterstereotypes from the outsider within experience and being positioned outside of hegemonic masculinity. These contradictions mean that interviewees have to rely on system 2 thinking, which Kahneman suggests requires engagement and agency in applying deliberate thought to making choices. Trans men do not outwardly reject masculinity but actively think about aspects of masculinity they want to emulate and those that they want to distance themselves from.

Primary to their decision-making process are their values and beliefs that underlie subprocesses involved in decision-making with self-direction and agency. In this chapter, I highlighted how trans men used this process in their decision-making about masculinity in their journeys to becoming men. Trans men were able to draw on their female histories to create a robust sense of self that can integrate their experiences and draw from them qualities which they think will serve them well as people. Connecting with their emotions, for instance, allows them to form deep connections with others. This connection with others—especially the women in their lives—has allowed them to challenge, and also affirm, their ideas of masculinity. In integrating their female histories into their sense of self, the trans men were able to develop a resilient masculinity that helps them withstand crisis.

This chapter illuminates the various cognitive processes that act together in trans men's construction of their masculine identities. From trans men's experiences of cognitive dissonance to their utilisation of masculinity as a heuristic, and later to their use of system 2 thinking, I demonstrate that the process of becoming men is agentic and purposeful. Trans men do not simply copy other men's portrayal of masculinity. Instead, they exercise their own value judgement in carefully and actively selecting those aspects of masculinity that they want to embody.

References

Allan, J. A. (2016). Phallic affect, or why men's rights activists have feelings. *Men and Masculinities, 19*(1), 22–41. https://doi.org/10.1177/1097184X15574338

Bandura, A. (1986). *Social foundations of thought and action: A social cognitive theory.* Prentice-Hall, Inc.

Bandura, A. (2001). Social cognitive theory: An agentic perspective. *Annual Review of Psychology, 52*(1), 1–26. https://doi.org/10.1146/annurev.psych.52.1.1

Barker, G. (2005). *Dying to be men: Youth, masculinities and social exclusion.* Routledge.

Barker, G. (2016). Male violence or patriarchal violence? Global trends on men and violence. *Sexualidad, Salud y Sociedad, Apr.*, 316–330. https://doi.org/10.1590/1984-6487.sess.2016.22.14.a

Butler, J. (2009). Performativity, precarity and sexual politics. *AIBR Revista De Antropologia Iberoamericana, 4*(3), 321–336.

Connell, R. (2005). *Masculinities* (2nd Edition). Polity Press.

Coston, B. M., & Kimmel, M (2012). Seeing privilege where it isn't: Marginalised masculinities and the intersectionality of privilege. *Journal of Social Issues, 68*(1), 97–111. https://doi.org/10.1111/j.1540-4560.2011.01738.x

Cromwell, J. (1999). *Transmen & FTMs: Identities, bodies, genders and sexualities.* University of Chicago Press.

Kahneman, D. (2011). *Thinking, fast and slow.* Penguin.

Kimmel, M., & Ferber, A. L. (2000). "White men are this nation": Right-wing militias and the restoration of rural American masculinity. *Rural Sociology, 65*(4), 582–604. https://doi.org/10.1111/j.1549-0831.2000.tb00045.x

MacInnes, J. (1998). *The end of masculinity: The confusion of sexual genesis and sexual difference in modern society.* Open University Press.

McMillan, A. S., & Paul, M. (2011). "It was good to learn how to show affection": Central American men who reject hypermasculinity. *Community, Work and Family, 14*(3), 367–382. https://doi.org/10.1080/13668803.2011.588050

Murray, G., Judd, F., Jackson, H., Fraser, C., Komiti, A., Pattison, P., Wearing, A., & Robins, G. (2008). Big boys don't cry: An investigation of stoicism and its mental health outcomes. *Personality and Individual Differences, 44*, 1369–1381. https://doi.org/10.1016/j.paid.2007.12.005

O'Neil, J., Wester, S. R., Heesacker, M., & Snowden, S. J. (2017). Masculinity as a heuristic: Gender role conflict theory, superorganisms, and system-level thinking. In R. F. Levant & Y. J. Wong (Eds.), *The psychology of men and masculinities* (pp. 75–103). American Psychological Association. https://doi.org/10.1037/0000023-004

Power, N. G. (2005). The "modern fisherman": Masculinity in crisis or resilient masculinity? *Canadian Women's Studies, 24*(4), 102–107.

Prati, F., Vasijevic, M., Crisp, R. J., & Rubini, M. (2015). Some extended psychological benefits of challenging social stereotypes: Decreased dehumanisation and a reduced reliance on heuristic thinking. *Group Processes & Intergroup Relations, 18*(6), 801–816. https://doi.org/10.1177/1368430214567762

Segal, L. (2001). The belly of the beast: Sex as male domination? In S. W. Whitehead Barrett (Eds.), *The masculinities reader* (pp. 171–194). Polity.

West, C., & Zimmerman, D. H. (1987). Doing gender. *Gender & Society, 1*(2), 125–151. https://doi.org/10.1177/0891243287001002002

8.   Conclusion

> **Abstract:** This is the concluding chapter of a study aiming to examine the decision-making processes that trans men in Malaysia utilise in constructing their masculine identities. The first stage saw trans men deal with cognitive dissonance arising from conflict between what they describe as their true selves and having been assigned female at birth. The second stage witnessed them proclaiming their male identities and performing masculinity for acceptance by other men. Cognitive dissonance led them to challenge ideas of masculinity and begin to think of their manhood beyond stereotypes and heuristics. They work out for themselves the kind of men they want to become without having to repudiate their female histories. They could do this without centring masculinity.
>
> **Keywords:** trans men, Malaysia, decision-making, becoming men, challenging masculinity

In embarking on this research project, I sought to answer the following question: What are the decision-making processes that trans men use to construct their masculine identities? In answering this question, I also wanted to explore from whom trans men learn about being men, the factors influencing the aspects of masculinity that trans men adopt, and the roles played by various institutions in the process of construction of trans men's masculine identities. The research findings indicate that the processes involved in decision-making on gender and expression lie in the intersections of the personal and political—familial, romantic, and social relations enmeshed with the various political histories and realities of Malaysian life—come together in an interplay of major and minor factors that require moment-to-moment reflection, reflexion, and action. Gender and expression are more than that which is determined by bodies.

The trans men I spoke to have also pushed me to think of being and becoming, and to question the assumptions I had made, perhaps from a position of cisgender privilege, about what being a man means. As a psychologist,

---

Kumaresan, Vizla. *Trans Men in Malaysia: Decision-Making, Masculinity and Manhood.* Amsterdam: Amsterdam University Press, 2025.

DOI: 10.5117/9789048562596_CH08

I was trained to think about identity formation as a time-bound project, depicted as stages, where the successful resolution of crises enables a person to develop psychologically and socially, with the successful outcome being stability. With such an idea of identity development, each of the stages of ego growth furnishes a necessary contribution to the resolution of the succeeding stage. Hence, identity development is successive and generative. This study's findings, however, suggest that interviewees' process of development as men is fraught with crises, but these are not necessarily markers of the stages of their development.

This realisation influenced my early thinking about decision-making processes and how I anticipated what the data would reveal to me. My early reading on the psychology of decision-making led me to expect a computation model influenced by symbols and systems (input and output) based on cognitive and probability theories. I was pushed to think beyond these models and ways of thinking about decision-making in light of trans men's narratives that challenged the idea of the process being linear. Trans men were not just passively responding to their internal processes or environment but were active agents in continually creating their environment and actions. Taking into consideration Bandura's (2001, p. 4) observation that "The human mind is generative, creative, proactive, and reflective, not just reactive," it becomes possible to imagine a more holistic model of decision-making that is cognisant of people's interpersonal factors and self-reflectiveness.

As such, it is only to be expected that the study brings forth various decision-making processes that trans men use with intentionality and reflexivity in the process of becoming men. Factors contributing to the choice of decision-making processes include self-interest (e.g. needing to blend in for personal safety), problem-solving (e.g. making quick decisions in social contexts), or creating ideas of what kinds of men they want or do not want to be (e.g. choosing anti-violence). In bringing these aspects together, in this concluding chapter, I will first provide a synthesis of the research findings before discussing the limitations of the study. Then, I will explore the impact of the study's research findings and avenues for future inquiry.

The narratives of 23 Malaysian trans men reveal a complex set of issues and processes that fall into three parts: before they transitioned, deciding to transition, and then transitioning to become men. While acknowledging that the process is not time-bound, I chose to present it in a stage model to demonstrate a literal sense of trans men's lives as ones that are emblematic of them *becoming* men. The motivating factor in trans men's decision-making process is cognitive dissonance, which they resolve by, first, using

CONCLUSION

masculinity as a heuristic and then system 2 thinking upon engaging their agentic selves in determining the kind of men they want to be.

Trans men's process of becoming men is one with a starting but not quite clear finishing line. Beginning at childhood, their gender expressions were always a painful negotiation between who they thought themselves to be—boys—and how the world perceived them—girls. This negotiation was tempered in various degrees by elders' tolerance within accepted gender norms, and various forms of social policing when these norms were presumed to be transgressed. The experience of disciplining was to ensure their bodies aligned with their gender expression, to exhibit appropriate sexual behaviour, and to eschew attraction for women while making themselves desirable to men. Men are perceived to be people whose romantic and sexual validation is needed but also to be feared as they inflict violence. This experience, for trans men, becomes crucial in developing their decision-making about their identities as men and their expression.

Trans men's coming out and transitioning processes do not happen in a step-by-step fashion; they experience coming out multiple times, in terms of gender identity and also sexuality. It is an evolving process dependent on the ongoing self-realisations that trans men experience. Decision-making here is reliant on factors that contribute to them being invisible as trans men and visible as men, allowing them the position of outsider within to observe intricate and minute details in their relationships with women and other men. Confronted with questions of "realness" due to their lack of a fully functioning penis and lack of sexual experience (perceived to be legitimate only if it is a penis penetrating a vagina), trans men are on the outside looking in to understand that an idea of masculinity built on competition for women and emotional detachment isolates them from their own experiences as men.

Inadvertently challenging ideas of masculinity and thinking of new ways of being and doing masculinity, trans men question male privilege from their ability to recognise the unearned biases they begin to receive because they are now men. The ensuing decisions that they make to create spaces for women in working towards equality at the workplace and home ironically expose them to negative consequences in terms of social punishment from both men and women. Realising the futility of measuring themselves against the standards of manhood that have been set by cisgender men, trans men apply their agency in deciding the kind of men they want to be, as well as the kind of men they do not want to be, and fashion their masculinity accordingly.

Primary to trans men's decision-making process are their values and beliefs that provide them a sense of self-direction and agency. Drawing on their female histories to create a robust sense of self that can integrate their experiences, they identify qualities which they think will serve them well as people. These include embracing their emotions, which allows them to connect with others and build intimacy in their relationships. This connection with others—especially the women in their lives—allows them to challenge and affirm their ideas of masculinity. In integrating their female histories into their sense of self, trans men develop a resilient masculinity that helps them withstand crisis.

Trans men's transitioning to become men highlights the value placed on the repudiation and rejection of the feminine that is perceived to be essential to being a man. The process of becoming men highlighted in this study demonstrates that the proximity of the feminine does not result in a crisis of masculinity. Instead, it is a catalyst to utilise more complex thinking and decision-making about being men and what that means. Trans men demonstrate that the process of becoming men is agentic and purposeful. While there is a place for mimicking other men's behaviours, the essential element in the processes of becoming men is the exercise of their own value judgement to carefully and actively select the aspects of masculinity that they want to embody. This involves an ongoing process of making and remaking what they think is essential to them becoming men. Crucial in their decision-making is the kind of men they want to be, a sense of gender justice, and the value that they place in connecting with themselves and others.

In utilising a grounded theory methodology, this study allows trans men to speak of themselves and for themselves to provide a holistic view of gender as they experience it in daily life. Doing this has also allowed this study to distance itself from the view of transgender mental health being primarily examined from a pathological perspective. While this study explores the role played by race in Malaysia in the construction of interviewees' masculine identities, I did not explore the role of language (Mandarin, Cantonese, Tamil, or Bahasa Melayu) and its impact on understanding concepts like masculinity to focus on decision-making in trans men's processes of becoming men. Language has an impact on identity formation where it builds conceptions of the self within religious, racial, and national identities. Future research could explore the intersections of any or all of these with that of gender identity.

This study demonstrates that trans men challenge the idea of binaric complementarity, thus delinking gender (masculinity) and sex (male). This poses a challenge to the idea that gender and sex exist in a binary relationship. In discussing nonbinary gender, Charlie McNabb (2018) problematises transitioning without an idea of another gender; i.e. how does one transition

CONCLUSION

if they are neither man nor woman? The findings in my book imply that one can be a man without being masculine and without having to denounce femininity, hence opening the possibility of various combinations of gender expressions and identities.

This study also challenges current ways of perceiving gender in the field of psychology. Echoing Sally Hines (2007), this study argues that identity may be experienced through gendered presentation and is not rigid, where the relationship between gender identity and presentation shifts and evolves through transition. Gender is not aligned with bodies, hence challenging current notions of examining gender expression in psychology. The complex intertwining of race, religion, and class in the postcolonial project that is Malaysia produces specific tensions around power, which plays out in gender identities, sexualities, and gender relations. It is my hope that this study can be used by trans men in Malaysia to better understand themselves and recognise the resilience and agency that they live out in their processes of becoming men and that they need not contend with questions of being man enough, thus alleviating any potential questioning of their male identities.

This book marks the end of my research project and the resolution of my identity as a PhD candidate. In doing this, I was able to reflect on my conflict between being a therapist and a researcher; mainly, in listening to interviewees describe their difficult experiences, I had to resist the therapist's urge to help them process these experiences and focus on being a researcher intent on gaining insights on my research question. My writing process was my attempt to insert the therapist in the researcher to help process these experiences for the interviewees as well as myself. Working on this project has informed my practice as a clinical psychologist and as a feminist. I now recognise the need to frame masculinities beyond the normative ideas of it and to recognise the different ways of expressing masculinities. Working towards more resilient frameworks of masculinities is an essential element of reframing gender relations and equality.

References

Bandura, A. (2001). Social cognitive theory: An agentic perspective. *Annual Review of Psychology, 52*(1), 1–26. https://doi.org/10.1146/annurev.psych.52.1.1

Hines, S. (2007). *TransForming gender: Transgender practices of identity, intimacy and care*. Policy Press.

McNabb, C. (2018). *Nonbinary gender identities: History, culture, resources*. Rowman and Littlefield.

Appendix

Analysing Interviews

Interviews were transcribed using Windows Media Player and an online tool called otter.ai. The online tool (otter.ai) was most useful when participants spoke slowly and with little Malaysian accent. The app was not adept at picking up Malaysian inflections, i.e. *lah*, the Malaysian tendency to speak fast, or more informal ways of speaking, i.e. "boobs." The transcripts were then sent to participants for member checking. I used NVivo12 to analyse the interviews. Each interview was divided into small sections of quotes. Each quote was then assigned codes. Quotes could have multiple codes assigned to them. Codes are derived from the findings themselves. NVivo refers to these as nodes. I read each quotation from the interviews and thought of the themes that they spoke to. These themes then became the nodes. Nodes are the smallest units of meaning of each quote. Each node (child node) is nested under a larger node (family node). I developed 24 family nodes and 424 child nodes.

Developing Chapter Outlines

The nodes informed the development of these chapters and how they flowed from one to the other. Interviewees' quotes were selected based on the nodes that corresponded to each chapter. I divided the research findings into three parts and six chapters. Each of the sections correspond to the different stages of interviewees' identities as trans men: pre-transition (Part 1: You're Not a Boy), deciding to transition (Part 2: I Am a Man, I Guess?), and transitioning (Part 3: I Know I Am a Man). Each of the chapters comprises two sections.

Index

accents   169
adolescence   38, 42, 48-49
affirmative action   134
agency   12, 28 n.7, 33, 63, 125, 137-138, 150-153, 157-160, 164-167
Ahmed, Leila   33
Alexis   49-50, 53, 62-64, 108-109, 148, 158, 159
anak dara   55
Anwar Ibrahim   10
appearance culture   49
Asher   50-51, 53, 155-156
Asian-Pacific Resource and Research Centre for Women (ARROW)   61
asylum   49
Australia   124-125
authority, male   15, 32, 36, 120-121, 128

Backus, Ron   129, 137
Bandura, Albert   12, 86-88, 125, 151, 153, 164
Barisan Nasional   10 n.9, 130
Barker, Gary   150, 158
Bartky, Sandra   32, 36, 57
beauty practices   47, 49-50, 57;   *see also* make-up
Ben   43, 50, 62-64, 128, 129, 137, 156, 158
binaric complementarity   47-48, 50, 57, 95, 149-150, 152, 154-155, 157, 158, 160, 166
Bird, Sharon   84, 103
birth certificates   *see* identity documents
bisexuality   63, 108
Black people   129, 137
Blue   27-28, 96-97, 101, 104, 105-106, 110-111, 144-145, 146
bodies   27, 38-39, 47, 55, 74, 79, 80, 83-85, 91, 99, 103, 120, 147, 155-156, 165, 167
control over   36, 56, 59, 60, 62, 73, 75
see also breasts; clothing; gender dysphoria; menstruation; puberty; surgery, gender-affirming; testosterone
body language   89, 110-111
bodybuilders   43
Bong, Sharon   10, 17, 82, 83
breasts
binding   42-43, 59-60, 79
and puberty   41-43
sexualisation of   42-43, 56
"bro code"   123-125
bromance   97, 101
Bumiputera   8, 134
Butler, Judith   31, 39, 82, 83-85, 156

capitalism   150
catcalling   103-104
Central America   150, 151, 153
Charmaz, Kathy   17

childhood   25-31, 86-87, 165
and play   27-31, 36, 76, 102
see also clothing, children's
Chindians   49, 126
Chinese Malaysians   8, 27, 30, 34, 43, 50-51, 59, 77-78, 86, 89-90, 126-128, 130, 135-137
Chou, Wah-Shan   72, 79
church   77, 88
circumcision   26-27
class   126, 155, 167
clothing
children's   26, 29, 33-36
female   41, 131, 159
baju kurung   52, 54
dresses   29, 34, 56
school uniforms   49, 52-53, 77
skirts   54, 56
underwear   42, 56
male   26, 34, 49, 79, 120
jippa   79
cognitive dissonance   11-12, 36-38, 40-44, 47, 64, 65, 71, 76-77, 152, 160, 164-165
colonialism   13, 15, 18, 33, 126-127, 129, 135, 137
coming out   41, 71-79, 82-83, 105, 120, 155
alternate models   72-73, 79
as a non-linear process   75, 77-78, 82, 165
as a Western construct   72-73
Committee on the Elimination of All Forms of Discrimination Against Women (CEDAW)   58, 133, 136
Confucianism   128-129
Connell, Raewyn   14, 95, 123, 126, 136-137, 148, 155
conservatism   10, 15, 78, 130
conversion therapy   9, 128
criminalisation   9, 123, 130
Cromwell, Jason   143
crying   102-103, 108, 146-147
Cunie   64-65, 88, 120-121, 132, 134, 157, 158

Damon   35-36, 56-57, 107, 118-119, 121-125, 129, 137, 145-146, 147, 148, 153, 155, 157, 158
dancing   84
Dante   31, 33, 41, 52-53, 78-79, 85
Deepavali   35, 79
depression   38, 41
Devor, Aaron   74, 76-78
Dines   39, 97, 101, 104, 107-109, 147, 148, 158
dolls   29, 30
Dorian   17, 32, 40, 79-82, 137, 158
driving   118-119

emotionality   97, 102-103, 146-148, 160, 165-166
empathy   64, 147, 154

families
  and acceptance 39, 73-74, 77-78, 105
  brothers 26, 51-52, 55, 59-60, 102-103, 146
  and coming out 72-74, 76-79, 105
  cutting ties with 78-79
  grandparents 32, 87, 90
  and messaging about gender 32, 34-36, 41, 44, 51-55, 105-106, 121-122, 128, 146-147, 156
  parents 34-36, 39, 40, 41, 51-57, 59-60, 63-65, 74, 77-78, 87-88, 90, 105-106, 122, 123, 128, 145-147, 153, 157
  sisters 52, 57, 73-74, 78, 102, 121-122, 146
fatwas 9, 134
fear 56-57, 59-61, 79-80, 99-100, 110
female histories of trans men 91, 95, 152, 154, 156, 159, 160, 166
feminism 16, 28, 62, 110, 147, 150
  male 145
  trans-exclusionary 109, 111
femininity 26, 29-33, 53, 87, 102, 146, 150, 152, 154, 159
  denying 84-85, 91, 96, 166
  disciplining into 47-57, 109, 148, 165
  emphasised/emphatic 14, 29
  and hierarchy 15, 32, 109, 144
  hegemonic 109
  male 108-109, 144-145, 148
  manja 105
  pariah 109
Festinger, Leon 11, 36-37
fishing 27, 30
Fiske, Susan 106, 110, 112
Flood, Michael 84, 86, 96, 99, 101, 103-104, 112
Foucault, Michel 36
freedom of movement 51-52, 57
friendships, trans men's
  with cisgender men 58, 86, 91, 95-99, 101, 104, 125
  with cisgender women 88, 98-99, 104 105, 107, 110-111
  growing up 30, 38, 52, 78
  with other trans men 158

Gabriel, Sharmani P. 126, 135
gay men 14, 122-124, 148-149
gender binary 15, 31, 42, 47-50, 72, 80-81, 84, 88, 95, 111-112, 144, 147, 148-149, 152, 154-155, 160, 166
gender dysphoria 38, 40-44
gender hierarchy 14-15, 31-32, 102-104, 109, 136
gender policing 32-33, 34-36, 39, 44, 47-50, 52-57, 80-82, 135-136, 165
  of oneself 83-84
  in toilets 80-82
  through violence 47-48, 55-57
gender role conflict (GRC) 11-12
Gene 77-78, 89-90, 105-106, 128, 129

genitalia 37-38, 44, 58-59, 101, 108-109, 111, 112, 155, 156, 165
Glick, Peter 106, 110, 112
Goh, Joseph 10, 13, 15, 17, 75, 82, 127, 133
Green, Jamison 25 n.2
grounded theory methodology (GTM) 17, 166
gyms 154

hairstyles 34-35, 49-50
Halberstam, Jack 15, 35, 76, 81, 109
Hall, Stuart 127, 137
handshakes 89, 130, 135
Hans 34, 37, 43, 55-56, 89, 119-120, 125, 135-137, 149-150, 153
heterosexism 15, 39, 109
heterosexuality 14, 38-39, 44, 57, 60-61, 72, 78, 90, 96, 99-101, 104, 124, 130, 133, 137, 148, 152, 158
heterosociality *see under* relationships
hijab 33, 36, 41, 52, 131
Hines, Sally 17, 167
homohysteria 97
homophobia 90, 124
homosexuality 10, 97, 123
  see also gay men; lesbians
homosociality *see under* relationships
honour 54, 57
housework 52, 55, 132
hormone therapy *see under* testosterone
human rights 7-8, 111
Human Rights Watch (HRW) 9, 10

identity-based motivation (IBM) 12
identity confusion 76-77
identity documents 25, 75, 82, 118, 127, 131-132, 143, 155-156
imperialism 15, 137
Indian Malaysians 8, 17, 28-29, 32, 35, 37-38, 39, 58, 79, 126-127, 129, 135-137
inequality
  gender 48, 81, 105-107, 109-112, 117-119, 132, 145, 157, 159-160, 165, 167
  social/structured 28, 117, 132-133, 150
  see also patriarchy
interfaith relationships *see under* relationships
Islam 8-9, 25, 26-27, 33, 48 n.1, 53, 127-128, 130, 132, 133-134
  conversion 131-132
  Islamisation 9, 10, 132, 133
  JAKIM 127-128
  Muslims 53-55, 57, 127-128, 130-133, 135-138
  Shariah laws 9, 130, 131 n.7, 132, 133-134, 136

Jake 30-31, 42-43, 52-53, 102-103, 104, 108, 147
JAKIM *see under* Islam
Jameel 26-27, 41, 79, 103-104, 123-125, 148-149, 158
Jankowiak, William & Xuan Li 128-129

INDEX

Jervind   59-60, 97-101, 104, 107-109, 157
John   58-59, 60, 74-76, 78, 137, 157, 158
Justice For Sisters (JFS)   10

Kahneman, Daniel   90-91, 152-153, 156, 160
Kelantan   130
Kimmel, Michael   81, 86, 159
Kyle   34, 63-65, 81, 120

labour
   and gender   9, 14, 52, 117, 119-122, 128, 133, 137, 159
   migration   129, 133
   and race   126, 135
   see also workplace
lasak   31, 33
LaudeB   28-29, 60-62, 73, 76, 77, 78, 129, 137
Lee, Julian   9, 10, 18
legal gender recognition   82, 108, 131, 143, 156, 157; *see also* identity documents
lesbians
   masculine   8, 38
   mislabelling of trans men as   38-39, 60, 73
   and trans male identities   53-54, 73-74, 77-78, 88, 89
Liw   81, 89, 130, 135, 137, 154, 158

MacInnes, John   159
*mak nyah*s   8
make-up   30, 41, 159
Malay supremacy   135-136
Malays   8, 9, 15, 26, 34, 49, 53-55, 57, 64, 89, 126-128, 130, 132-138
Malaysia
   languages   166
   laws   9, 10, 55, 82, 108, 123, 127, 130, 131-134, 136, 143, 156, 157
   sociopolitical context   8-10, 13, 15-16, 18, 25, 26, 27, 33, 59, 106-107, 126-138, 163
   women's movement   110, 133-134, 136
marriage   72, 108, 131-132, 133, 136
masculinity
   and aggression   62, 90, 124, 129, 145-146
   Black   137
   Chinese   128-129
   and competition/competitiveness   60, 98, 103-104, 124, 129, 165
   complicit   14
   crisis   159, 166
   and decision-making   11-13, 16, 18, 36, 48, 57, 58, 61-65, 72, 84, 86-91, 112, 118, 125, 144, 146, 150-154, 157-160, 163-166
   distance from femininity   91, 96, 98-99, 103, 123, 136, 144, 148-150, 152, 159, 166-167
   embodying   13-14, 83-91, 153, 157-158, 160, 166
   emotional detachment   102-103, 104, 146, 165
   female   9, 15, 35, 54-55, 81, 109, 112, 144, 154, 159

financial provision   105-106, 128, 157, 158
hegemonic   14-15, 18, 103, 104, 109, 123, 126, 132, 136-137, 144-145, 148, 150, 153, 155, 158, 160
   and heterosexuality   99-101, 104, 148, 158
   as a heuristic   11, 31, 65, 85-88, 90-91, 95, 112, 118, 144, 150, 151, 152, 154-155, 160, 165
   and hierarchy   14-15, 81, 86, 99, 102-104, 109, 124, 128, 136-137, 155-156
   Malay-Muslim   15, 132-138
   and maleness   13-15, 144, 149, 154, 157, 159, 166-167
   marginalised   14-15, 137, 155
   and power   15, 36, 90, 104
   resistant   158
   role as protector   31, 33, 63, 103-106, 149-150
   stoicism   146-147
   subordinated   14-15, 123, 129, 137, 148
   toxic   90
   in trans children   25-35
   white   137
massage parlours   97-101, 104
mateship   124-125
McMillan, Anita and Moli Paul   146, 147, 150-151, 153
McNabb, Charlie   166-167
medicalisation   7, 17
menstruation   102; *see also* puberty
migration   129, 135
Miles   49-50, 83-85, 88, 101, 108, 110-111, 147, 148, 154, 158
misogyny   60
Mitch   17, 53-54, 56, 87-88, 110, 130-132, 134-135, 137, 146, 158
Mohamad, Maznah   132-133, 136
money   105-106
morality policing   130-131, 133
mosques   130-131
Muslims   *see under* Islam

nation-building   15-16, 18
naturalness   25-26, 28, 31, 35, 50, 53, 76, 80, 82, 148-150
nonbinary gender   166-167
norms
   cultural   53-55, 61, 129
   gender   13, 15, 43, 48-53, 57-58, 64, 75, 81-82, 84-85, 89, 101, 118-119, 156, 165

O'Neil et al   11-12, 31, 65, 85, 90, 150
objectification of women   42-43, 56, 59, 62-63, 96, 104
Ong, Aihwa   54, 55, 133
outing   80, 108-109
outsider within   117, 138, 160, 165

pak nyah   8 n.6
Parti Islam SeMalaysia   130
passing   72, 81-83, 91, 95, 130, 156

pathology 15, 17, 166
patriarchy 9, 12, 14-15, 33, 36, 51, 55, 57, 60, 64, 118-119, 121, 123, 129, 133, 136, 138, 145, 150, 159
Pease, Bob 121-122, 124-125
pedestal effect 120, 145
Peletz 132-133
pengkid 8, 54-55, 120
People's Voluntary Anti-Homosexual Movement (Pasrah) 10
perspective taking 63-64
police 118-119
polygamy 133, 136
postcolonialism/postcoloniality 13, 18, 126-127, 167
power relations 9, 15, 51, 57, 60, 65, 87-88, 91, 104, 121-122, 150, 155, 167
privilege
    Bumiputera 134
    cisgender 163
    female/feminine 106, 109-110, 111
    male/masculine 14-15, 17, 51, 117-125, 128, 133, 138, 145, 159, 160, 165
    pronouns 37, 58, 73, 75, 77, 96-97, 104, 107, 156, 159
psychology 15, 18, 28, 29 n.9, 36, 163-164, 167
PT Foundation 8
puberty 34-35, 37, 40-44
    breast development 41-43
    menstruation 40
public spaces 58-59, 89, 103, 111
    women's and girls' access to 51
    see also toilets

race 8, 14, 18, 25, 126-127, 132, 134-137, 155, 166, 167
racism 129
Rao, Rahul 13 n.15, 16, 127
'real' men 81-82, 99-100, 104, 108-109, 112, 117, 155, 165
relationships
    heterosocial 104, 112
    homosocial 84, 95-98, 101-103, 112, 121, 124-125, 129, 145-146
    interfaith 131-132
    romantic 105-108, 118, 121-122, 124, 131-132, 134, 145, 147, 148-150, 152, 154, 157, 158, 163
religion 15, 25, 88, 126, 127, 130-134, 137, 166, 167
    and LGBTQ identities 54, 88
    see also church; Islam; relationships, interfaith
Rubin, Henry 34, 38, 41-43

safety 10, 32, 62-64, 72, 79-83, 88, 89, 91, 103, 110, 124, 156, 164
Schilt, Kristen 14, 81-82, 117, 120
Schippers, Mimi 109, 112
school 28, 31-32, 38-39, 40, 43, 49, 50, 60, 105
    all-girl 38, 156

co-ed 40, 49, 77
    primary 31-32, 43
    religious education 54
Section 377A 123
Selangor 33, 134
self-harm 43-44
sex 8, 25, 30, 123
sexism 99, 107
    benevolent 106-107, 109-110, 112
    hostile 106, 109-110, 112
sexual harassment *see under* violence
Shah, Shanon 123, 127, 130
Shane 17, 85-86, 110-111, 124-125, 158
Shariah laws *see under* Islam
Singapore 128-129
Sisters in Islam (SIS) 33, 134
social cognitive theory 12
social learning theory 86-89
social ostracisation 38, 123
socialisation
    as female 33, 38-39, 47-57, 122, 143
    as male 97, 121-122
sodomy 10
sports 30, 42, 51, 135-136, 149, 158
"stealth" 10
stereotypes 12, 48, 57-58, 65, 90, 100, 104-107, 109, 112, 117-119, 121-122, 129, 135, 138, 144-147, 150, 154-155, 157, 160
    counter- 154-155, 160
Stryker, Susan 16
surgery, gender-affirming 7, 9, 75, 83, 97, 99, 111, 155
system justification theory (SJT) 106
systems theory of cognition 90-91, 152-153
    system 1 thinking 90-91, 153
    system 2 thinking 91, 152-154, 156-157, 160, 165

tegur 131
Teh Yik Koon 7-8
testosterone 16
    hormone therapy 13, 74, 77, 84, 97, 120, 134, 146, 155
toilets 79-83, 111-112
tomboyism 34-35, 42, 54-55, 74, 76
touch, physical 97, 135
    non-consensual 99-100
trans women 7-9, 10, 16, 111, 117
    and women-only spaces 111-112
transitioning 14, 58, 71-84, 89, 91, 96-98, 104-105, 110-111, 118, 120, 134, 144, 148-149, 153, 155, 164-167
    economic constraints 41, 75, 82-83
    legal 14, 82
    medical 71, 74-75, 77, 80, 82-84, 96-97, 134, 155-156, 157, 159
    social 58, 71-75, 82, 120
"transsexual" 7-8

INDEX 175

United Malays National Organisation
(UMNO) 10
United States of America 97, 123, 129
urination 29, 32, 36

violence
domestic 35-36, 55-57, 59, 63-65, 90, 107,
121, 122, 133, 145-146, 157
gender-based 47-48, 55-65, 80-82, 110-112,
119, 124, 131, 133, 150, 156, 159
and masculinity/men 12, 63, 80, 103-104,
112, 124-125, 129, 149-151, 159, 165
as natural 149-151
rejecting 149, 153-154, 158, 159, 164
sexual 51, 56, 58-63, 90, 99-100, 103-104, 111,
131, 138, 149, 150
state 119, 123, 130, 156
vigilante 10
virginity 55

visibility 17, 165
voices, trans men's 80, 83, 96-97

welfare 9
West, Candace 30-31
Westbrook, Laurel 81-82, 110-111
Westernisation 9, 127, 137
White Lotus 37-39, 123-125, 146, 156, 158
white people 33, 137
women's movement *see under* Malaysia
workplace 14, 77, 96, 103-104, 108, 117, 119-121,
138, 154, 165

Yogyakarta Principles 7-8, 26, 111
Young, Iris Marion 40, 42, 53

Zimmerman, Don H. 30-31, 52, 144
Zonneveld, Ani 130